natural fabrics

natural fabrics

SIMPLE AND STYLISH SOFT FURNISHINGS

IAN MANKIN AND GINA MOORE

SPECIAL PHOTOGRAPHY BY NADIA MACKENZIE

EBURY PRESS
LONDON

First published in the United Kingdom in 1997 by Ebury Press
Random House, 20 Vauxhall Bridge Road, London SW1V 2SA

Random House Australia (Pty) Limited
20 Alfred Street, Milsons Point, Sydney, New South Wales 2061, Australia

Random House New Zealand Limited
18 Poland Road, Glenfield, Auckland 10, New Zealand

Random House South Africa (Pty) Limited
Endulini, 5A Jubilee Road, Parktown 2193, South Africa

Random House UK Limited Reg. No. 954009

A CIP catalogue record for this book is available from the British Library.

ISBN 0 09 182020 0

Editor: Emma Callery
Design: Alison Shackleton
Special Photography: Nadia Mackenzie
Stylist: Nicole Albert
Illustrations: Kate Simunek
Picture Research: Nadine Bazar

Colour reproduction by Colourpath
Printed and bound in Singapore by Tien Wah Press

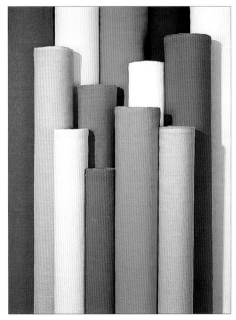

contents

*'At some point you realize there's only one way to
do something, and it's very simple. Some people
never achieve simplicity. Most people.'*

LOUIS MALLE

introduction

I have often been asked the question, 'Why natural fabrics?', and recently I came to realise that in a lot of what I do, I am trying to re-create my past. It comes naturally to me since I have come from an era when you had cotton socks in summer and woollen socks in winter, Aertex vests and Harris Tweed jackets, proper leather shoes, worsted suits, as well as linen sheets, hand-embroidered tablecloths with drawn-thread work and napkins to match, and tapestry chair covers. Man-made fibres simply did not exist then in our day-to-day lives.

Through all the years that I was in the leather trade, I was dealing in natural products – skins and trimmings such as horn buttons, pure wool linings, solid brass fittings and wood framed cases for the luggage (even my backing buttons were mother-of-pearl).

Textiles have been in my family background for several generations. My father had a wholesale textile business in Soho, London, and I found a listing for it not long before he closed that described it as: 'An old-fashioned shop with an original wooden counter and a wholesale-looking window display ... Largely a wholesaler who buys direct from the mill, Louis Mankin gets constant and changing bargains in natural fabrics. The shop is a reliable source of cheap heavy-duty denim, unbleached calico and hessian, shirting and butcher's stripes.' There is no doubt that this was the germ of the idea for my shop.

My influences are down-to-earth. I dislike pretentiousness and I want my shops and the fabrics in them to be simple and honest. It is an uncomplicated approach to things, using craftsmen to make the shop fittings and running the business in a way that cuts out all the frills such as accounts, credit cards and computers.

I choose the fabrics that I feel represent good value and are timeless. I don't forecast and I don't follow fashion. The criteria I use when choosing new fabrics are that I like to feel that I could use or live comfortably with everything we stock and that having made a purchase from us, no one would say some months later, 'What on earth made me buy that?'.

A favourite author of mine said, 'I can't afford to take myself seriously. I hope to entertain, that's all.' Well, I don't think I'm out to entertain, but a friend of mind once said about my previous business, 'You give pleasure to people'. I like to feel that I still do.

masook

masook

HANKS OF BRIGHTLY DYED FABRIC
HUNG OUT TO DRY IN THE FIERCE
INDIAN SUN.

'On a visit to India some years ago, I remember standing on a balcony that ran all the way around a central courtyard, looking down on the dyed yarns, in all these wonderful colours, spread out in the sun to dry. I took lots of photographs to remember them by, but when I had the film developed, it came back totally blank. Nevertheless, I carried those colours in my head and we still stock many of them today.'

Masook is not a specific textile term. Instead, it is simply a rather romantic sounding name derived from the Hindi word for 'lover'. It is given to plain, yarn-dyed, tightly woven, hand-loomed Indian cotton repp. This is a heavily corded fabric where the ribs run across the fabric.

The tight structure of Masook was initially developed in the early 1960s in a response to a request by Liberty's of London for a tightly woven, furnishing-weight fabric. There are 80 warp threads to the inch where previously the maximum number had been 60. This tight structure gave the fabric, which Liberty called Reptrust, the strength and quality that enabled it to be successfully marketed in the West as a furnishing fabric.

Masook is made in Cannanore, in Kerala, a green and beautiful state on the south-west coast of India. Also known as the Malabar coast, Cannanore has a wild and romantic past with spice trading links to the West that pre-date the arrival of Vasco da Gama from Portugal in 1498. It is a region that has a fine tradition of high quality textile production.

Indeed, cotton textile production in all of India has an incredibly long and fascinating history, some understanding of which helps to explain its worldwide success today. The cotton plant is indigenous to India, and it is thought that it became the first region in the world to develop techniques for processing the ripe cotton bolls into yarn. Those who grew it also learnt to dye cotton fibre with fast dyes some 3,000 years before such techniques were developed in Europe.

Europeans were enraptured by the colourful cloth they found in India and a flourishing trade was established at least as early as the fifteenth century.

The dyers of India belonged to a specific and quite lowly caste. But that has enabled their long-established expertise to be handed down from generation to generation in an unbroken chain. A dyer at work today can pick up a pebble from the ground and use it to mix what are usually chemical dyes in a bucket to match any given colour with extraordinary intuitive accuracy.

Another reason for the beauty and subtlety of Indian colours is that the cotton yarn is always dyed before it is woven. In contrast, fabric in the West is invariably piece-dyed which leads to a uniformity of colour throughout the cloth. The slight irregularities of colour in yarn-dyed cotton, together with the uneven, slubby texture produced by the hand-spun and hand-loom process, result in a cloth of unrivalled ethnic charm.

In the nineteenth century, at the height of British rule in India, the Indian textile industry suffered from an influx of cheap, machine-made cloth from the mill towns of Lancashire, designed specifically for the Indian market. In the struggle to achieve independence from the British between 1915 and 1947, Mahatma Gandhi used the domestic weaving industry as a vehicle to bring home the reality of commercial domination by foreign rulers. 'Khadi', meaning hand-spun, hand-woven cloth, became the symbol of homespun independence and self-sufficiency. After Independence in 1948, the Khadi programme revived and reinvigorated the hand-loom industry of India, and so grew India's status as a major textile exporter today.

A ROUGH WOODEN SHELF UNIT CAN BE TRANSFORMED BY DRESSING IT UP WITH A MASOOK COVER. ATTACH THE FABRIC ALL AROUND THE TOP OF THE UNIT WITH VELCRO AND WHERE IT MEETS AT THE FRONT, STITCH ON TWO PRETTY BOWS. THEN FIT A SCALLOPED COVER OVER THE TOP.

USING MASOOK

Masook was especially developed as a furnishing-weight cloth and is therefore well suited to upholstery and loose covers, as well as possessing the draping qualities necessary for curtains. The extent and charm of the Masook colour range is its strongest attraction. These colours, though they are no longer made with vegetable dyes, have not lost the soft, natural characteristics that are associated with those older processes. As a result, the Masook colours seem to sit well in today's interiors, where we have come to value the intrinsic qualities of natural materials and hand-craftsmanship.

So, if you are looking for a colour palette that ties-in with the warm tones of a wooden floor, or with an exposed brick or stone wall, you will find it in Masook. You need look no further if you are trying to marry the dusty terracottas and deep blues of an Oriental rug to the colour scheme of your other furnishings. If you already own some antique or ethnic textiles – perhaps tapestry cushions or a quilted throw – Masook colours will always work well with them.

Try putting together contrasting colours: border your curtains with one, or even two, contrasting colours; pipe loose covers and upholstery with another colour to emphasize the shape; or pile cushions in a variety of toning colours onto a deep, comfortable sofa. You will find that the Masook colours come to life when not used in isolation.

There are also Masook checks and stripes that coordinate with the plain shades, expanding the range of possibilities for unusual and stunning colour combinations. Pick out a colour from the plain Masooks that matches your dinner service and use it to make a serviceable tablecloth for your dining table. But if you then go on to border it in a check fabric in a colour that matches, say, the colour of your dining-room walls, you will successfully tie the whole together and create a harmonious dinner setting.

A MASOOK THROW

When Ian Mankin decorated his first flat in his early twenties, his passion for stripes was already apparent. Not being able to find the stripe he wanted, he bought two bolts of plain cloth and sewed them together in wide stripes to make up pillow cases and a throw to arrange along the length of a divan bed. The throw in the pictures opposite and overleaf was inspired by that idea, and shows how a plain fabric is made much more exciting by simply combining two or more colours.

opposite CONTRASTING COLOURED STRIPS OF MASOOK ARE SEWN TOGETHER TO MAKE A STRAIGHTFORWARD AND STRIKING THROW, FIT FOR ANY LIVING ROOM.

Cut strips of two contrasting colours of Masook into equal widths and machine them together to create a striped throw. Line it with a solid backing in one of the plain colours, and then bind it with a neatly mitred border in a third colour. As a smart finishing touch, run lengths of embroidery silk in running stitches along the seams of the stripes through to the plain backing. This is more than purely decorative – it holds the two layers together as one.

MASOOK – THE PRACTICALITIES

• Masook stretches along the warp (its length) when it is machined, which means that the tightest of loose covers are sometimes hard to achieve. Likewise, when measuring the finished length of a pair of curtains you must be careful not to stretch the cloth as you measure or you may end up with them being shorter than you intended. At the same time, especially with very long curtains, they may drop in length over time when hung. So don't rush to alter them if they seem too short when you first put them up.

• Those wonderful subtle colours will fade if exposed to direct sunlight. To prevent this from happening, always line curtains and blinds, and protect upholstery that has to be placed near a sunny window.

• Being 100 per cent cotton, shrinkage has to be allowed for if the item Masook is made into is to be washed rather than dry-cleaned. Never tumble dry it, and replace loose covers that have just been washed when they are still slightly damp so that the fabric has a chance to stretch back to fit.

• For the same reason, when making up curtains, don't use a heavy steam iron to press in the turnings and open the seams – the steam will shrink the cloth very slightly and you will be forever mystified as to why the sides of your curtains twist when hung. Always use a dry iron (actually this is good advice when making up any cloth into curtains).

---

previous page THESE CUSHIONS HAVE BEEN MADE FROM A VARIETY OF FABRICS BUT THEY ARE UNIFIED BY THE NEUTRAL, UNDERSTATED TONES.

opposite THE TERRACOTTA SHADOW-CHECKED MASOOK USED TO UPHOLSTER THE SOFA IN THIS AIRY AND ORDERED LIVING ROOM ADDS TO THE GRIDS FORMED BY THE PICTURE FRAMES AND THE CONSERVATORY ROOF.

pleated cushion cover

PREPARATION

- From main colour, cut piece A measuring 43 x 153 cm (17 x 60 in).
- From contrast colour, cut piece B measuring 23 x 53 cm (9 x 21 in) and piece C measuring 63 x 53 cm (25 x 21 in).

FINISHED SIZE
50 x 50 CM (20 x 20 IN)

YOU WILL NEED

- 1.6 M (1¾ YD) MASOOK IN MAIN COLOUR

- 0.6 M (24 IN) MASOOK IN CONTRAST COLOUR

- 4 BUTTONS

- 50 x 50 CM (20 x 20 IN) CUSHION PAD

- CHALK OR PENCIL

- RULER

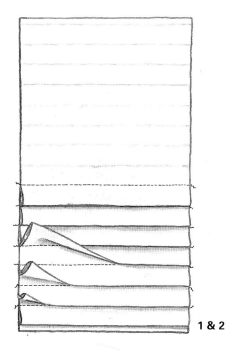

1 & 2

1 On the long sides of A, mark the pleat lines every 5 cm (2 in) and leaving 1.5 cm (⅝ in) allowances at the top and bottom.

2 Bring every third pleat line down to meet the first pleat line, and stitch across the top of each pleat (10 in all). Continue until you have a piece of pleated fabric measuring 53 x 43 cm (21 x 17 in).

3 Take B and with right sides together lay one long edge along one pleated edge of A and, leaving a 1.5 cm (⅝ in) seam allowance, stitch together and press over to B. Press in a 1.5 cm (⅝ in) hem along the other long edge of B and fold in towards the seam. Slipstitch down.

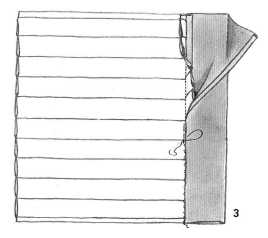

3

4 Stitch a narrow double hem along one short edge of C (this will make the pocket flap of the cover when folded back).

5 With right sides together, lay A/B onto C so that the pleated edge of A is along the unhemmed short edge of C, and the hemmed edge of C extends beyond the folded edge of B. Fold C back over the top of B, and stitch around three sides of the cover through all the layers.

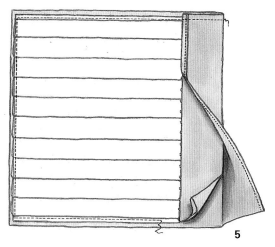

5

6 Turn the right sides out. Make four buttonholes on B and sew buttons in corresponding positions onto C.

footstool

From a foam-rubber supplier, order a cube of firm quality, fire retardant foam measuring 46 cm wide x 46 cm deep x 38 cm high (18 x 18 x 15 in). You then have to make a tightly fitting inner cover out of lining.

There are two reasons for this – to facilitate putting on and removing the loose cover, and as the lining is made to fit tightly, it pulls in the edges of the foam, slightly rounding off the shape of the footstool.

PREPARATION
- Cut lining as follows:
  2 pieces, each measuring 93 x 38 cm (40 x 15 in) for the sides
  2 pieces, each measuring 46 cm (18 in) square for the top and bottom.

- Cut the main colour of Masook as follows:
  1 piece measuring 49 cm (19 in) square for the top
  4 pocket pieces, each measuring 28 x 36 cm (11 x 14 in)
  2 side pieces, shaped and measured as in the diagram on page 23

- Cut the contraast colour of Masook as follows:
  2 m (2 yd) bias-cut strip 5 cm (2 in) wide for piping (see page 118)
  4 pocket binding pieces, each measuring 7 x 36 cm (2¾ x 14 in)

YOU WILL NEED

- 1.25 M (1⅛ YD) LINING

- 2 M (2 YD) MASOOK IN MAIN COLOUR

- 1 M (1 YD) MASOOK IN CONTRAST COLOUR

- PIPING CORD

- CHALK

- 1.75 M (1¾ YD) OF 12 MM (½ IN) WIDE TAPE CUT INTO 8 EQUAL LENGTHS

1 Sew together the two long pieces of the lining at both ends with 1 cm (½ in) seam allowances. With right sides together, pin and machine the bottom section to the sides, taking a 1 cm (½ in) seam allowance and clipping into the corners. Press in 1 cm (½ in) around the top edge of the sides and slide the lining onto the foam cushion. Press in 1 cm (½ in) around the edge of the top section, pin to the sides and stitch with strong cotton.

2 Make up the piping in the contrast colour (see page 119) and sew it all around the top section of the main fabric. Sew the side sections together with right sides facing and with 1.5 cm (⅝ in) seam allowances. With right sides together, pin and then machine the top section to the sides, taking a 1.5 cm (⅝ in) seam allowance and clipping into the corners. Using chalk, mark your pocket positions, as indicated on the diagram on page 23.

2

3 Make a 1 cm (½ in) hem along one long edge of a pocket binding piece and machine. With right sides together, lay the opposite raw edge of the pocket binding along the top edge of a pocket piece and, taking a 1.5 cm (⅝ in) seam allowance, machine them together and then press the seam open. Turn under all the raw edges around the whole pocket by 1.5 cm (⅝ in) and press. Turn the pocket binding over to the wrong side leaving a 1 cm (½ in) stand of pocket binding at the top of the pocket, and slip stitch the binding on the wrong side.

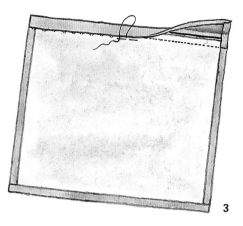

3

securely at either end. Then, again top stitch along the bottom edge, catching in the pleat at both ends.

6 Press in and machine a 1 cm (½ in) hem all along the bottom of the cover, being careful not to stretch the semi-circular cut-out shape. Sew tapes to each corner securely with a square of stitches.

7 Put the cover onto the cube and tie it tightly beneath. Pleat the excess fabrics at the corners and hold them flat with a few tacking stitches that are easy to remove when washing the cover.

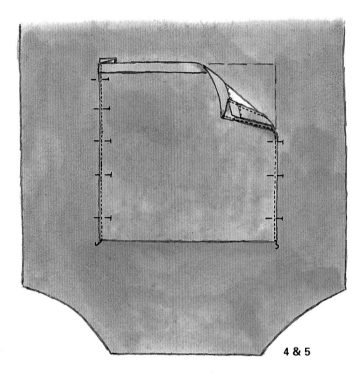

4 & 5

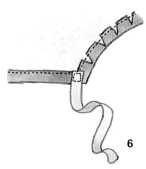

6

4 Now make a 2 cm (¾ in) wide pleat down each side of the pocket, press and then top stitch down the edge of each pleat to hold the pleats in place. Repeat for the other three pockets.

5 Pin the pockets in position on the right side of the cover. Top stitch down the two outside edges, back stitching

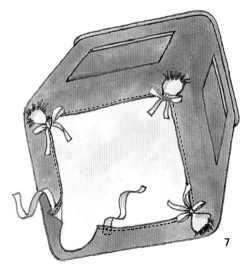

7

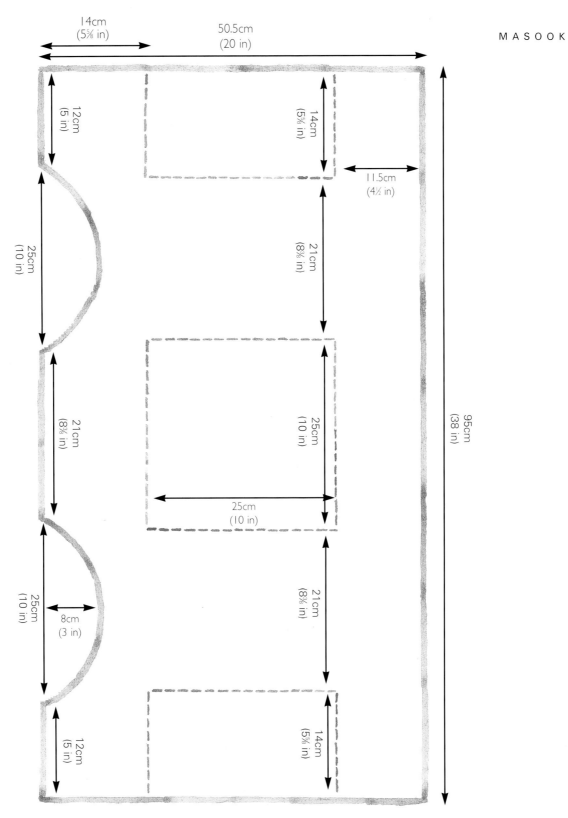

14cm
(5⅝ in)

50.5cm
(20 in)

12cm
(5 in)

14cm
(5⅝ in)

11.5cm
(4½ in)

25cm
(10 in)

21cm
(8¼ in)

95cm
(38 in)

21cm
(8¼ in)

25cm
(10 in)

25cm
(10 in)

25cm
(10 in)

8cm
(3 in)

21cm
(8¼ in)

12cm
(5 in)

14cm
(5⅝ in)

Cut two pieces like this and mark pocket positions in chalk

pleated border curtains

These curtains have a deep, horizontally pleated contrast border along the bottom, and a delicate linen fringe has been attached to hide the seam line. The depth of this border should be the measurement from the windowsill to the floor, or, if it is a French window, up to a fifth of the overall length. Measure up your window (see pages 120-1) and decide on the number of drops needed and the depth of the border.

PREPARATION

- Cut the main colour of Masook to the length of the overall drop less the depth of the border plus 11.5 cm (4½ in) x the number of drops required.

- Cut the contrast colour of Masook to the depth of the border plus 10 cm (4 in) for each horizontal pleat plus 21.5 cm (8½ in) x the number of drops required.

- Cut the lining to the finished length of the curtain plus 15 cm (6 in) x the number of drops required.

- Cut the linen fringe and gathering tape to the overall width of the curtains before they are gathered.

- If you are using more than one drop per curtain, sew them together. Then sew the deep contrast border to the upper part of the curtains, taking a 1.5 cm (⅝ in) seam allowance.

YOU WILL NEED

- MASOOK IN MAIN COLOUR
- MASOOK IN CONTRAST COLOUR
- LINEN FRINGE
- LINING
- 2.5 CM (1 IN)-WIDE GATHERING TAPE
- CURTAIN HOOKS

1 Lay out one of the curtains wrong side up on a flat surface. Press in a 5 cm (2 in) hem down both sides. Herringbone stitch down the sides of the curtain to within 20 cm (8 in) of the bottom edge. Press in a 10 cm (4 in) double hem along the bottom of the curtain, mitring the corners neatly (see page 122). Open the bottom hem out again.

2 Decide where the horizontal pleats will be placed and how deep each one will be. Draw the first pleat line across the wrong side of the curtain with chalk where the top pleat will fall. Measure 10 cm (4 in) down from this line and draw another line. Draw the remaining pleat lines as on the diagram to the right. Fold the pleats by bringing each lower line up to meet the top line, pin and press. Then machine and repeat for each subsequent pleat.

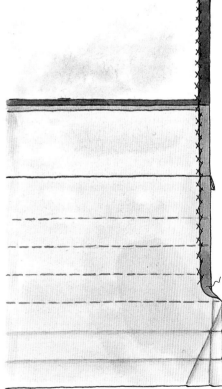

1 & 2

3 Re-fold the bottom hem, attach covered penny weights at the corners and at the bottom of the seams (see page 122), and slip stitch the hem.

4 Turn the curtain over to the right side to attach the linen fringe. Lay the fringe along the seam line, pin and tack neatly in place. At each side of the curtain, turn the ends of the fringe over to the wrong side of the curtain and continue tacking to the edge of the side hem. Tuck the ends of the fringe back under the side hem and sew securely so that it cannot unravel.

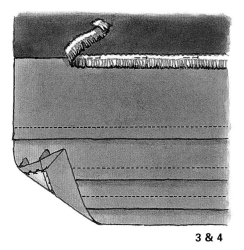

3 & 4

5 Sew the lining drops together if you are using more than one drop per curtain and press open the seams. Press up a 5 cm (2 in) double hem along the bottom and machine. With wrong sides together, lay the lining onto the curtain with the bottom of the lining 5 cm (2 in) up from the bottom of the curtain, and aligning the curtain and lining sides.

6 When you are sure the lining is lying quite flat and straight on the curtain, press under the sides of the lining to within 2.5 cm (1 in) of the side of the curtain. Slip stitch the lining down the sides, carrying your stitches on about 5 cm (2 in) around the bottom corner of the hem. Finish off securely.

7 Measuring up from the bottom of the curtain, mark the finished length along the top of the curtain with pins. Press over the excess fabric along this pinned line. Mark a line 7 cm (2¾ in) down from this fold line with chalk. Machine on the 2.5 cm (1 in)-wide gathering tape (see page 123), placing the top of the tape along this chalked line. Repeat steps 1 to 7 for the other curtain.

5, 6 & 7

utility

utility

STRIPED DECK CHAIR CANVAS IS
THE PERFECT EXAMPLE OF A
UTILITY FABRIC DESIGNED
SPECIFICALLY FOR THE JOB. IT
IS EXCEEDINGLY STURDY,
BRIGHTLY COLOURED FOR THE
BEACH OR GARDEN, AND IS
ONLY WOVEN TO THE WIDTH OF
A DECK CHAIR FRAME.

'One of the most interesting things I've seen was the use of navy and white butcher's stripe. It's a very strong-looking stripe, but one of our customers decided to use the reverse side and created a wonderful subdued effect rather like a city gent's chalk stripe suit. It's applying lateral thinking to fabrics.'

It could be argued that most of the fabrics in the Ian Mankin range are utility fabrics. The very germ of his idea was to take fabrics that already existed and were traditional, functional and natural, and call them Ian Mankin. From the early days, his shops always stocked such workaday stalwarts as butcher's stripe, linen scrim, ticking and even Aertex. The fact that these fabrics were not traditionally used for interiors was the contradiction that put a contemporary spin on his idea.

In the years that have followed, he has developed the ticking range to such a degree that it warrants a chapter of its own (see pages 56-69). So it is left to canvas and calico to carry the utility mantle.

The name for canvas derives from the early English word 'canevas' which, in turn, derives from the Latin for hemp – cannabis. It was from hemp and flax that early heavy, closely woven fabrics were made that were used for tents and sails. Nowadays, the term canvas refers to a cloth more usually made from cotton, with a great variety of uses which are often indicated by a prefix such as artist's canvas, embroidery canvas, Royal Navy canvas or deck chair canvas, the salient feature of all being their strength and firmness. It comes in various weights ranging from the practically see-through lightweight through to a workmanlike heavyweight. There is even a hand-spun, hand-loomed Indian canvas in a range of vibrant colours.

Calico derives from Calicut, a port on the beautiful south-west coast of India where a plain, woven, cotton cloth was made. The East India Company used to collect fabrics from here to trade in the spice islands further east. It was often printed and, indeed, in America, the term calico is more commonly associated with cotton fabric with a small printed pattern. Nowadays, it describes a plain, woven, carded cotton cloth usually unbleached with the characteristic small, dark flecks of the cotton seed. It is often sized to give it more strength and body and to make it moisture resistant. Among other things, calico is used as the undercloth in upholstery and for making toiles or dummy patterns in the tailoring industry.

Calico is now being sold washed and pre-shrunk so that the sizing has been completely removed. This means that the fabric is no longer stiff and is more suitable for making softly draped curtains.

USING UTILITY FABRICS

Heavyweight canvas is a strong, dense cloth, eminently suitable for tight upholstery and sturdy loose covers, although it ought to be pre-washed for the latter. It will make up into heavy, cream Roman blinds which won't need to be lined, and if it is not used too full, will drape well for curtains.

Use canvas with detailing that harks back to its utilitarian past – punch metal eyelets into the top of a canvas curtain and tie it to the curtain pole with rope. You could even forget the pole and simply hook the eyelets onto a row of hooks above your window,

holding the curtain back with a rope. Searching through the hardware and ropes in a boat chandlery will prove inspiring when thinking of a surprising way to hang canvas curtains and blinds.

Lightweight canvas is a sturdier alternative to muslin. You can use it to screen an ugly view, while still letting light into a room by using it to make unlined blinds. Or make summer-weight, unlined curtains to billow at an open French window by gathering it generously onto narrow gathering tape and consider binding the curtains on all sides with a pretty, bias-cut check.

HEAVYWEIGHT CANVAS HAS BEEN USED TO LAVISH EFFECT AS CURTAINS AND PRETTILY TIED CHAIR CUSHIONS IN THIS CLEAN AND ELEGANT INTERIOR.

The Indian canvas has the characteristic slub of hand-spun cotton, but the even weave still makes for a sturdy and stable cloth. Yarn-dyed in vivid colours from burnt orange to a clear turquoise, they are a colourful addition to the utility range. Make up a cushion in each of the jewel colours with a buttoned flap closing and place them together on a pale cream sofa to lift an otherwise neutral setting.

Calico is a cheap and versatile cloth. In its original, heavily-sized form, it is sometimes difficult to work, although it makes up into rather wonderful, sculptural curtains if used generously on a large scale. The sizing makes it water repellent – it is still used to make protective dustsheets – so you could use it for loose fitting chair covers, perhaps to protect more valuable fabric beneath. However, remember that the sizing washes out with repeated laundering.

Washed and pre-shrunk, calico becomes a soft, unbleached, unpretentious cloth which will gather into simple, unlined curtains for a cottage interior, or become something else entirely if it is thickly interlined and lavishly swagged over a pole. Calico's greatest asset is that it is very cheap, so using it imaginatively and generously will not break the bank. Pleated and affixed to the wall with brass studs is a fairly inexpensive, but striking, way of walling a room and certainly cheaper than re-plastering, and when you grow tired of the look, or the fabric becomes too dust laden, it is cheap enough to discard.

THE LOOSE COVERS FOR THESE TWO IMPOSING WINGED ARMCHAIRS HAVE BEEN MADE FROM CALICO. IN EARLIER TIMES, IN THE LARGE HOUSES OF THE ARISTOCRACY, CALICO DUST COVERS WERE USED TO PROTECT VALUABLE UPHOLSTERY WHEN ROOMS, OR EVEN WHOLE HOUSES, WERE CLOSED FOR THE SEASON.

A CANVAS KITCHEN BLIND

Canvas seems a natural and utilitarian choice for a kitchen. Teamed with dyed herringbone webbing you can make this simple roller blind in less than an hour. Bear in mind, however, that the blind needs to be rolled up by hand, so use it at a window that you can reach easily, or where it is unlikely to be moved very often.

You will need fabric cut to the size of your window plus 10 cm (4 in) extra in the width, and at least 12 cm (4½ in) extra in length; two lengths of dyed herringbone webbing (see page 119) each about twice the length of the blind; a broom handle cut to the width of the blind, and a batten of 5 x 2.5 cm (2 x 1 in) timber cut to the width of the window.

Turn in 1 cm (½ in) and then 5 cm (2 in) down each side, and machine. Roll the bottom edge of the blind onto the broom handle and glue it into position and then nail it with small tacks so that it can't unroll. Wrap the other end of the blind around the batten of wood, and staple or nail it into position.

Fold the two lengths of webbing in half and staple them to the top of the batten of wood equidistant from each end, so that one end hangs down the back of the blind, and one end down the front. Now attach the batten to your window frame, using 4 cm (1½ in) right-angled brackets or by simply drilling right through the fabric and batten and screwing directly to the wall or frame. Roll up the blind by hand to the height where you would like it to hang, and tie the webbing into a simple knot or pretty bows, depending on which look you prefer.

UTILITIES – THE PRACTICALITIES
• All these utility fabrics are 100 per cent cotton and, unless they are labelled 'pre-shrunk', will shrink when washed. Artist's canvas is designed to shrink so that it will stretch tightly over a frame to make a flat surface on which to paint. It is therefore important that when something is likely to be washed and not dry-cleaned, the fabric is washed before being made up; or you must make up your curtains longer than required, to allow for shrinkage.

• Canvas is very stable, but calico tends to stretch. It sometimes has a wavy selvedge where it has been stretched in the manufacturing process. Where this is the case, it is necessary to cut a straight edge before making up curtains, as a wavy edge will never hang straight.

opposite CANVAS AND DYED HERRINGBONE WEBBING MAKE A BEAUTIFULLY SIMPLE BLIND, BOTH TO MAKE AND TO LIVE WITH.

squab cushions

YOU WILL NEED

- 75 CM (30 IN) PACIFIC STRIPE FOR EACH CUSHION INCLUDING PIPING

- 1.2 M (48 IN) OF 2.5 CM (1 IN)-WIDE NATURAL HERRINGBONE TAPE OR WEBBING

- 375 G (12 OZ) POLYESTER WADDING

- SPRAY ART AND CRAFT ADHESIVE

- PIPING CORD

1 First make a template of the seat of your chair on newspaper, marking where the uprights of the chair back meet the seat. Add a 1.5 cm (⅝ in) seam allowance all around the template and use it to cut two cushion shapes from your fabric. Mark the positions of the chair uprights on the fabric with chalk. Also cut one cushion shape, without the seam allowance added, in wadding. Cut enough 5 cm (2 in)-wide strips to make piping to go around the outside of the cushion.

2 Using spray glue, glue the wadding to the underside of one of the fabric cushion shapes. From the right side of the fabric, machine through the fabric and the wadding along the edges of each stripe so that you have a quilted effect.

3 Make up the piping and then machine the piping to the edge of the quilted cushion shape (see page 118), leaving a 1.5 cm (⅝ in) seam allowance.

4 Cut the herringbone tape into two equal lengths. Fold each length in half and pin the folded ends into position where you have marked the position of the uprights of the chair back. Machine stitch back and forth a few times across the folded end of the tapes to make sure they are securely anchored.

5 With right sides facing, machine together the two cushion shapes, leaving an opening of about 15 cm (6 in) at the back of the cushion. Turn the cushion right side out, press it flat and hand stitch the opening to close it. Tie the cushion onto the chair seat and trim the tapes to the required length.

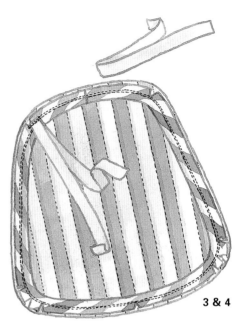

3 & 4

5

kitchen curtains

To work out how much fabric you will need, see Measuring up on pages 120-1. Because these curtains are pleated at the top they need to be exactly twice the width of the pole, so, if necessary, cut down the width of your fabric to fit, bearing in mind that you will be adding a wide contrasting border down the leading edge. In this case, because the pole was 130 cm (51 in) wide, each curtain (including the border) needed to be 130 cm (51 in) wide. So, after deducting the 15 cm (6 in) width of the border for the leading edge, the plain canvas had to be 115 cm (45 in) plus 5 cm (2 in) for the outside edge hem and 2 cm (¾ in) seam allowance. So the canvas had to be cut to 122 cm (48 in) in width by the required length which included 20 cm (8 in) extra on the bottom for the hem and 5 cm (2 in) turning at the top. The border was cut to the same length and twice its finished width plus 4 cm (1½ in) for seam allowances.

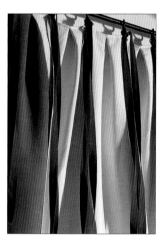

YOU WILL NEED

- HEAVYWEIGHT NATURAL CANVAS

- PACIFIC PLAIN COTTON FOR BORDER

- CURTAIN LINING

- 6 LEAD PENNY WEIGHTS

- CHALK

- 2.5 CM (1 IN) WIDE HERRINGBONE TAPE

- FABRIC DYES (OPTIONAL, SEE PAGE 119)

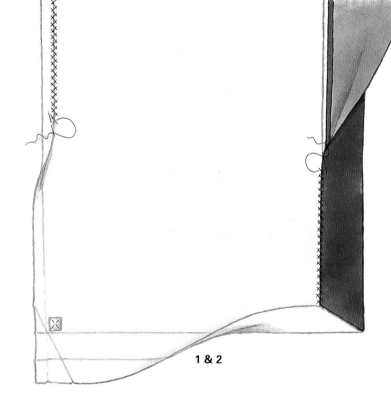

1 & 2

1 For each curtain, pin the contrasting fabric border to the canvas along the leading edges, right sides together and raw edges aligned. As the Pacific Plain has more 'give' in it than the canvas, be careful not to stretch it. Stitch together the two fabrics with a 2 cm (¾ in) seam and press open. Turn up a 10 cm (4 in) double hem along the bottom edge, and a 5 cm (2 in) hem on the canvas edge.

2 Turn in the border fabric so that it meets the seam. Mitre the bottom corners (see page 122) tacking a covered penny weight into each corner (also see page 122). Tack another weight at the bottom of the border seam (and any other seams if you are using more than one drop) and slip stitch the hem. Herringbone stitch by hand down the canvas side hem, and down the border side.

3 Machine stitch a 5 cm (2 in) double hem along the bottom of the lining. Lay the lining onto the curtain with wrong sides facing and with the canvas edge of the curtain aligned with one edge of the lining, and the bottom edge of the lining lying 5 cm (2 in) above the bottom edge of the curtains.

4 Cut the lining to fit the curtain so that it overlaps the stitched edge of the border by 4 cm (1½ in). Turn the lining under 2 cm (¾ in) on each side and slip stitch down the side seams. Stitch around the bottom corners for a short distance.

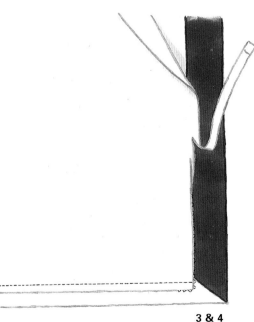

3 & 4

5 Now, measuring up from the bottom hem, mark the finished length of your curtain across the top with a line of pins. Press over the excess fabric along this line. Trim down the fabric and lining to 2 cm (¾ in) above this line. Remove the pins, turn in the raw edges towards each other and press.

6 Now work out the spacing for your ties. They should be spaced about 10 cm (4 in) apart on the finished width of the curtain. So if the finished width of each curtain is to be 70 cm (28 in), divide that by 10, and you have seven sets of ties. Divide the measurement across the top of the unpleated curtain by six and you will have the distance between your seven ties. Mark those positions with chalk.

7 Cut the tape into seven lengths of 130 cm (51 in), fold each in half and tuck the folded end into the curtain top at each of the marked positions and pin.

8 To work out your pleats, take the finished width of the curtain (70 cm [28 in]) away from the unpleated width (130 cm [52 in]) and divide that figure (60 cm [24 in]) by the number of pleats (six). The figure you get (10 cm [4 in]) is the width of each pleat. Make a 10 cm (4 in) inverted pleat in the middle of the space between each tie, and pin in place.

9 Machine stitch right across the top of the curtain very close to the edge, making sure that the tapes and pleats are all securely caught. You will have to change the colour of the thread in your machine to stitch across the border.

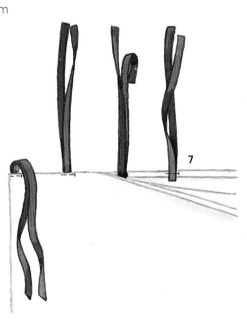

7

linen

linen

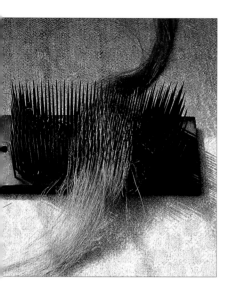

TO REMOVE THE STRAW HUSK
FROM FLAX, THE FIBRES ARE
PULLED THROUGH A BED OF
NAILS. THIS TECHNIQUE IS
KNOWN AS HACKLING.

'On a recent trip to one of our distributors in Copenhagen, I wandered through the old part of the city and I spotted an antique shop window full of the most wonderful old mattress coverings. I went into the basement and there, piled floor to ceiling, was the most amazing assortment of old linen covers, some of which still had feathers attached to them. It was hard to choose between them and I spent quite some time deciding which one to reproduce.'

When Tutankhamen's tomb was opened in 1922, linen curtains which had been there for about 3,250 years were found intact. The Egyptians also used linen to make the mummy cloths in which they wrapped their dead, and mummy cloths have been found that date back 4,500 years. These amazing facts are testimony to linen's unique strength. It was not so much that other textile fibres were not in use then, so much as they have not survived the passage of time to tell the tale without rotting.

Linen is made from flax, and the age-old process by which flax is converted to spun yarn has always been extremely labour intensive and was never suited to mechanization. This is why flax lost much of its importance as a textile fibre after the development of the cotton gin in 1793. Here was a machine that separated the fibres from cotton seeds and spurred the massive industrialization of cotton production. However, wherever there is a demand for the particular qualities pertaining to flax, linen is still very evident.

Flax is stronger than cotton, and when it is wet, it is 20 per cent stronger than when it is dry. This explains why linen was often used for the production of sail and tent canvases in the past, and marine ropes made from flax are still used today. Another characteristic is that it is a good conductor of heat which is why linen sheets feel so cool and linen garments are comfortable to wear in hot weather. In fact, when one considers that linen is cool, looks good, is entirely natural and survives repeated laundering, it is not hard to understand why it makes an appearance on the international fashion catwalks every summer season. To designers in the fickle world of fashion, wedded to the idea of built-in obsolescence, linen's only drawback must be that one of their garments might just last as long as King Tutankhamen's curtains.

Linen blended with cotton at the weaving stage is called union cloth and was developed as an upholstery fabric. It is a cloth that encompasses the best characteristics of linen – its strength and lustre – but is made both more malleable and more cheaply by being woven with 50 per cent cotton. It comes in varying weights, from a lightweight curtain linen union to heavier, upholstery weights.

Century Stripe was developed to imitate a remnant of linen mattress ticking that was over a hundred years old. The yarn composition and herringbone weave were relatively simple to copy, but in order to faithfully reproduce the original, a way had to be found to age the new fabric. This was done by dying the yarn for the coloured stripes in hanks by a method called space dying which transfers the colour unevenly and, once the yarn is woven, creates a distressed effect.

USING LINEN

Linen is used extensively as a furnishing fabric, again principally because of its strength. Plain, woven, 100 per cent linen in various weights is manufactured, and often printed, for the top end of the furnishing market. Linen scrim is an open mesh, plain, woven cloth made from heavy, rough, uneven yarns and used in the upholstery trade, but is sometimes used to make lightweight curtains. Linen sheeting is woven 2.4 m (8 ft) wide and, apart from the bed linen for which it is intended, can be made into marvellous billowing,

THE CLEAN LINES OF THIS MODERN, LINEN-COVERED SOFA HAVE BEEN EMPHASIZED BY PARING DOWN THE STRUCTURE OF THE UPHOLSTERY TO A MINIMUM. PIPING ON ALL SEAMS HAS BEEN OMITTED, LEAVING ONLY THE LUSTRE OF THE LINEN TO DELINEATE THE SHAPE.

unlined curtains. Linen also comes as a lightweight muslin which is more opaque and a stronger alternative to cotton muslin.

All the linen unions are extremely good value for upholstery fabric and their traditional and timeless qualities work well with antique furniture. Conversely, if used in a contemporary setting, they seem to take away some of the shock of the new, to look as though they have always been there. A deeply buttoned seat cushion in Century Stripe on an old Windsor chair, for example, will not look inappropriate in any way. As tight upholstery on an antique sofa, it will roll back the years.

Linen union is not the same as the linen traditionally used for bed linen, but you can make a throw-over bedcover in a heavy union cloth and simply fray the edges where they rest on a bare wooden floor. Hang linen drapes or a Roman blind at the window, again perhaps with the bottom hems frayed, and then make a pile of linen-covered floor cushions – some striped and some plain.

A LINEN TABLE SETTING

To make the tablecloth, place mats and napkins like the ones in the serene table setting overleaf is a deceptively simple task that requires practically no sewing. In each case, work out how big you want them to be, including the fringing, and, in the case of the place mats, including a 1.5 cm (⅝ in) turning along the top and bottom edge. Cut out each piece of fabric, following the grain as carefully as possible. To help you, pull a thread out of your fabric across the width of the fabric and cut along the resulting line. Machine with a very small zigzag stitch along the sides at the point where you want the fringe to start. Then, starting at the outside edge, fray the edges to within a thread or two of your zigzag stitch line.

opposite AN ANTIQUE CAMPAIGN BED HAS BEEN GIVEN A NEW LEASE OF LIFE WITH DEEPLY BUTTONED BOX CUSHIONS COVERED IN A SMART, BLACK STRIPED LINEN.

overleaf SEAT COVERS, ROMAN BLINDS AND SIMPLE CURTAINS EACH MADE FROM CENTURY STRIPE LINEN BRING A SMART AND COORDINATED FEEL TO THIS DINING ROOM.

LINEN – THE PRACTICALITIES

• Linen is another fabric that seems to look better after repeated laundering as its sheen and polish improve with age. However, it shrinks quite a lot (about 10 per cent) so it is advisable to wash it before making up if it is being used for something that will be washed rather than dry-cleaned. Do not tumble dry.

• Linen can crease badly, so press it when it still retains about 50 per cent of the moisture and, after ironing, hang it up to finish drying.

seat covers

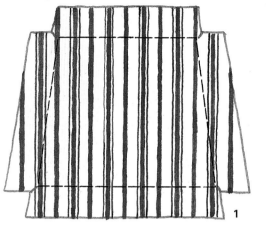

YOU WILL NEED

• 0.5 M (½ YD) CENTURY STRIPE FOR TWO COVERS

• 1 M (1 YD) OF 2.5 CM (1 IN)-WIDE HERRINGBONE TAPE FOR EACH COVER, DYED TO MATCH IF NECESSARY (SEE PAGE 119)

1 Make a template of your seat shape on paper. Add 5 cm (2 in) (or whatever you need to cover the depth of the seat on your chair) to all four sides, and then 1.5 cm (⅝ in) for turning allowance. Cut your fabric to match the template and snip into the seam allowance on the inside corners.

2 To reinforce the corners at the uprights of the chair back, cut two squares of cloth about 6 cm (2½ in) square. Fold these across to form two triangles and tuck in the raw edges neatly.

3 At the back of the seat cover, fold in the seam allowance first 5 mm (¼ in) and then 1 cm (½ in). Pin a reinforcing triangle in position across the corners so that the raw edges of the hem are covered. Pin one end of each of the four ties into position, 1.5 cm (⅝ in) in from the four outside corners.

4 Machine the hem close to the inside folded edge across the end of the tie and the reinforcing triangle, turning a right angle and onto the other folded hem. Machine diagonally across the corner.

5 At each front corner, pin the fabric together with right sides facing and machine a 1.5 cm (⅝ in) seam. Snip into the fold at the top of the seam and then press open.

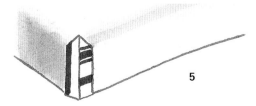

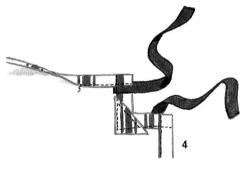

6 To make a hem along the back edge of the cover, fold in 5 mm (¼ in) and then 1 cm (½ in) and machine it close to the inside folded edge, back stitching at either end across the ties. Make a hem around the rest of the cover in the same way.

roman blind

YOU WILL NEED

- MAIN FABRIC IN CENTURY STRIPE
- LINING FABRIC
- 2.5 CM (1 IN) HARDWOOD EDGING STRIP
- VELCRO (SEW AND STICK) THE WIDTH OF THE BLIND
- HOLLOW BRASS RINGS (3 PER ROD POCKET)
- 9 MM (⅜ IN) DOWELLING ROD THE WIDTH OF THE ROD POCKETS BY THE NUMBER OF POCKETS
- 5 x 2.5 CM (2 x 1 IN) SOFTWOOD BATTEN
- SAW
- HEAVY-DUTY STAPLE GUN
- 4 SCREW EYES
- TWO 4CM (1½ IN) ANGLED BRACKETS
- ROMAN BLIND CORD
- ACORN OR CORD WEIGHT
- SMALL BRASS CLEAT

PREPARATION

- Cut the fabric to the size of the blind plus 5 cm (2 in) all the way around for turnings.
- Cut the lining to exactly the size of the blind plus 5 cm (2 in) allowance in the length.
- Cut rod pockets from the lining to the width of the blind and 10 cm (4 in) wide. To work out the number and position of the rod pockets, see below.

WORKING OUT THE POSITIONS OF ROD POCKETS

- First decide on the number of folds you want in the blind and then take the finished length of your blind and subtract 10 cm (4 in). Divide this figure by twice the number of folds plus one. This will give you the distance from the bottom edge of the blind to the first rod pocket.
- The other rod pockets are positioned at twice this distance.
- The last rod pocket will have twice this distance plus the 10 cm (4 in) you subtracted at the beginning of the calculation between it and the top of the blind. (The 10 cm [4 in] stops the rod pockets catching on the screw eyes when the blind is raised.)
- Mark the position of the rod pockets on the lining by drawing a line in pencil across the width of the lining. Ensure that the lines are very accurately drawn, evenly spaced, and fall at right angles to the side seams.

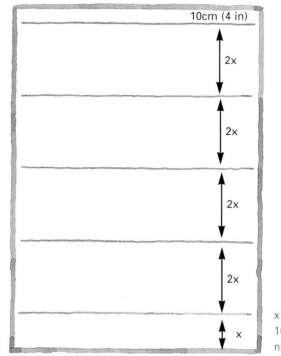

x = (finished length – 10cm [4 in] ÷ (2 x number of pleats + 1)

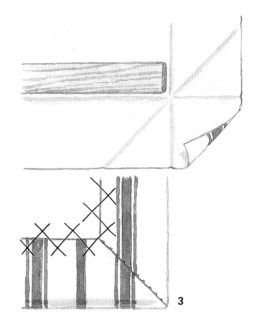

1 To make each rod pocket, fold in 2 cm (¾ in) at one short end of a pocket piece and then fold it in half lengthways and press. Next fold in a 1 cm (½ in) double hem along the raw edges, press and machine close to the inside edge of the hem. Then fold in a 1 cm (½ in) double hem at one end and machine down that end and along the length of the pocket close to the outside edge of the hem.

2 Pin the rod pockets to the lining, with the folded edge of the pockets along the pencil line on the lining, leaving 2 cm (¾ in) at either end where the lining will be folded in. Carefully machine in place as close as possible to the folded edge of each pocket and back stitch securely at either end.

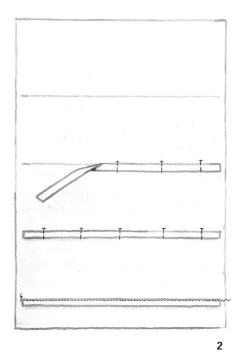

3 Press in a 5 cm (2 in) hem along the sides and bottom edge of the face fabric, mitring the corners (see page 122). Cut a piece of the hardwood edging strip to fit inside the hem along the bottom of the blind. Lay it in place and catch the hem down all the way around the sides and the bottom with herringbone stitch. With wrong sides together, lay the lining onto the blind fabric and turn under 2 cm (¾ in) of the lining sides and bottom. Slip stitch in place and press.

4 Lift the flap of each rod pocket and, as close as possible to where it is attached to the lining, run a strong double thread picking up a tiny bit of the face fabric every 8-10 cm (3-4 in) across the width of the blind.

5 Measure up from the bottom of the blind the length you require and mark the top of the blind with pins. Cut away excess fabric 2 cm (¾ in) above the pins, fold over and press. Attach the soft side of Velcro across the top with two rows of machine stitching.

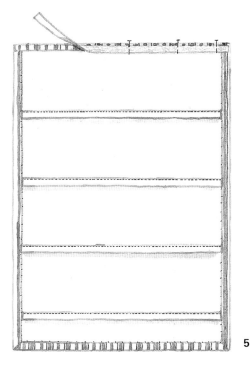

5

8 Staple the other, hard, side of the Velcro to the front edge of the batten. Then attach the batten to the window frame, or the wall above the window, with the angled brackets.

9 String up the blind by tying a cord to each of the bottom rings, threading it through all the rings above it. When the blind is attached to the batten, pass the cord through the screw eye above and across through the other screw eyes, including the extra one towards the side where the cords will hang down.

10 Pass all the cords through the cord weight or acorn, check that the blind is pulling up level, and then knot the cords together and cut off any surplus. Attach the cleat to the wall at an appropriate position for winding the cord.

6 Mark with pencil on the rod pockets the points where the brass rings will be sewn on: 8 cm (3 in) in from each outside edge, and one in the middle. Sew on the brass rings with strong thread (making sure they are securely anchored as they have to take quite a bit of strain). Insert the dowelling rods.

7 Make up the fixing batten by cutting a piece of the planed softwood to fit the width of the blind, less 1 cm (½ in). Using the staple gun, cover it neatly with your face fabric. Into the underside of the batten, put in the screw eyes 8 cm (3 in) in from either end, and one in the middle. The fourth screw eye goes 2 cm (¾ in) in from the side where the cords will hang down, usually the right.

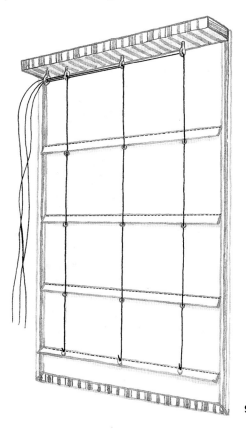

9

7 & 8

ticking

ticking

'All the classic fabrics that I've reproduced have been linked to some kind of reminiscence or memory. As part of a brief, but very good, boarding school education that I loved, it was insisted that we made our own beds every day, complete with hospital corners and turning over the mattress which was made of black and white ticking. To this day I still own a mattress with that self-same ticking.'

The word ticking comes from the Latin 'theca', meaning a case or cover, for that was what it was always used for – the covers of mattresses, bolsters and pillows. Other names for ticking in the past were bedstout, inlet and bedtick.

Traditionally, ticking was a stout cotton cloth tightly woven in a combination of thick and thin stripes in a twill or herringbone weave. The stripes were most commonly black and white, although in Victorian times it was sometimes woven in red and white too. As it was necessarily a cheap and functional cloth, it was usually woven with a single warp thread which was strengthened by being dipped in a solution of flour and water, or starch, and that had the added bonus of making the finished fabric more feather proof. It also made the finished fabric as stiff as a board, but while its purpose was simply to cover mattresses that was not regarded as a disadvantage.

Ian Mankin's name is synonymous with ticking. It was one of the traditional and utilitarian cloths that he stocked in the very early days of the shop in Primrose Hill, but he found that in its original, starched form, its applications were limited. For the first time he began to think about having a fabric specially woven and when he found an unusual batch of grey and white ticking in a mill in the north of England the idea of using other colours provided another incentive to develop what was almost a totally new fabric.

To overcome the problem of maintaining strength, the ticking was woven with a double warp thread so that some of the size could be omitted, and, in the finishing process, it was washed and scoured with softening agents. The result was a fabric that looked exactly like the original tickings, but felt and behaved in a very different way. Still strong enough to be used for upholstery, it could now lend itself to loose covers and curtains as well.

The colour range started conservatively enough with a sage green and a Wedgwood blue, both of which were combined with a natural, unbleached background, rather than a stark white. Since then, the range has grown to encompass 17 colours of which air force blue is probably the most popular, and several different stripes, of which the newest and most sophisticated is the Empire range.

In the process, ticking has established Ian Mankin as a major force in the field of furnishing fabrics, with his timely gift for transforming something that is traditional and everyday, making it distinctive and contemporary.

USING TICKING

In keeping with its original function, ticking makes an excellent upholstery fabric. The tightly woven herringbone structure retains the intrinsic strength that was primarily developed to encase feather mattresses. It also has a timeless quality that lends itself as well to the upholstery of modern pieces as to antiques. In fact, ticking seems to particularly lend itself to blending the old with the new.

Use it to upholster an elegant antique chaise longue, and it will not look out of place in an otherwise cool contemporary decor. Conversely, used to cover a stark modern chair, it will provide a softer link to other, older pieces in the room. Such timelessness is a useful tool for today's eclectic tastes.

For the same reasons of strength and stability, ticking can also be used for loose covers. Again, its very familiarity seems to convey comfort, ease and informality – attributes that everyone would want to bestow on their favourite sofa.

Ticking looks at home in a bedroom. Use it to make a bed valance to cover the

THE SIMPLEST CHOICE FOR A CONSERVATORY HAS BEEN MADE HERE WITH THE USE OF ROLLER BLINDS MADE UP IN A GREEN TICKING STRIPE.

59

bed base, and then make, or have made, a deep-buttoned bed head in ticking. It is too heavy a fabric to use for making the actual bed linen, but there is plenty of scope for a quilted bed cover or throw. Bond a sheet of ticking to a thin layer of polyester wadding, quilt it very simply by machining along the stripes, and then bind it to a backing layer with a neat contrast border in a plain colour. If the style you are seeking, however, is less restrained and formal, and you have the time and dedication to undertake the making of an heirloom, ticking, with its wide range of stripes, checks and colours can be used in endless combinations to make traditional patchwork quilts. To complete the bedroom, pile big cushions on the bed covered in a variety of coordinated tickings.

For window treatments, ticking is especially suitable for blinds because of its stable weave structure. Also, there is something about stripes in general that seem to suit the simple lines of both roller and Roman blinds. Roller blinds can be made of ticking, either by applying stiffener to the fabric, or by laminating it to a stiff backing. Try putting roller blinds made of a simple ticking stripe behind curtains in a more complicated stripe, or perhaps another plain cotton fabric such as a calico or Jacquard stripe.

The innovation of removing the starch from traditional ticking has created a fabric that hangs beautifully and looks wonderful made up into curtains. If your ceilings are low, stripes help to add an illusion of height to a room, especially if used for long

A BUTTONED FOOTSTOOL, LONGER AND WIDER THAN ONE EXPECTS, HAS BEEN UPHOLSTERED IN BLACK AND WHITE TICKING AS THE CENTREPIECE IN A GARDEN ROOM. THE MONOCHROME STRIPE IS ECHOED IN THE LINES OF THE WROUGHT IRONWORK AND THE WINDOW FRAME.

curtains. You can interline them for a more formal, and luxurious feel, deeply pleating the heading with hand-made triple-pleating, but ticking suits today's trend towards simpler curtains. Make them up with a looped heading, and then hook back, perhaps with a loop sewn on two thirds of the way down the leading edge, to reveal a contrast lining in another ticking.

THE TICKING STUDY

In this study (see previous page, opposite and overleaf), simple but effective ideas have been employed using fabric to add a little style to otherwise dreary office equipment. Using double-sided tape and the thinnest polyester wadding, you can turn the most mundane plastic-coated file into an item that might actually make filing a pleasure!

To make a pleated lamp shade, you will need two wire rings, the smaller one with a light bulb clip attached. The best source for these is an old lamp shade. Remove the old shade material and measure the circumference of the larger ring. Make a rectangle of thin card, as deep as the lampshade you require, and as wide as your circumference measurement plus 6 cm (2½ in). Using spray fabric glue, cover it with ticking and pleat every 2 cm (¾ in) across the width of the rectangle. Make holes with a hole punch through each pleat, 2.5 cm (1 in) from the top edge.

Glue together the short sides of the rectangle, thread a cord through the punched holes, and draw up the pleats tightly at the top of the shade. With the shade upside down, open out the pleats at the bottom, position the large metal ring just inside the edge and superglue in place. Rest the smaller metal ring near the top of the shade and superglue in position. You should only use this shade with a low-wattage light bulb.

TICKING — THE PRACTICALITIES

• Despite its stable structure, ticking is made from 100 per cent cotton and may shrink very slightly when washed. So, in the case of loose covers make them up fashionably loose, adding 3 per cent to your measurements.

• As a hard-wearing fabric, ticking takes repeated washing well. In fact, the more it is washed, the better it looks. Use a cool wash on a short cycle, and on no account tumble dry as it is heat that shrinks cotton.

---

previous page INSTEAD OF SIMPLY SEAMING TOGETHER TWO PIECES OF THE SAME FABRIC TO MAKE A BLIND WIDE ENOUGH TO COVER A WINDOW, USE CONTRAST BORDERS CREATIVELY TO MAKE A UNIQUE STATEMENT.

opposite CARDBOARD FILE STORAGE BOXES PURCHASED FROM AN OFFICE EQUIPMENT SUPPLIER CAN EASILY BE COVERED IN FABRIC USING DOUBLE-SIDED TAPE TO HIDE THE INEVITABLE ACCUMULATION OF PAPERS AND CLUTTER.

unstructured blind

As an alternative to a straightforward Roman blind, this particular design is unstructured and has no rod pockets attached to the lining at the back. When pulled up, soft folds are formed rather than the crisp pleats of a Roman blind. Because of this, the blind has to be arranged when you pull it up, so use it either on a window that is low enough for you to reach, or where you are unlikely to want to pull the blind all the way up and therefore out of reach, if, for example, there is an ugly view outside.

First measure up the window (see page 120). Then decide how wide the borders will be. The pleats should be about 15 cm (6 in) deep, and the bottom border needs to be deeper so that it shows when the blind is pulled up. To help decide on the proportions, make a scale drawing on paper.

Buy enough brass rings so that you can sew them about 30 cm (12 in) apart on either side of the blind from the top of the bottom border to within 30 cm (12 in) of the top of the blind.

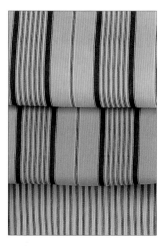

YOU WILL NEED

• MAIN FABRIC
(HERE EMPIRE 1)

• TICKING CONTRAST A
(HERE TICKING 1)

• TICKING CONTRAST B
(HERE TICKING 2)

• LINING FABRIC

• VELCRO (SEW AND STICK)

• 16 MM (⅝ IN) HOLLOW
BRASS RINGS

• 9 MM (⅜ IN) DOWELLING
ROD THE WIDTH OF THE
CENTRAL PANEL LESS 6 CM
(2½ IN)

• 5 x 2.5 CM (2 x 1 IN)
SOFTWOOD BATTEN THE WIDTH
OF THE BLIND

• SAW

• 3 SCREW EYES

• TWO 4 CM (1½ IN) ANGLED
BRACKETS

• ROMAN BLIND CORD

• ACORN OR CORD WEIGHT

• SMALL BRASS CLEAT

PREPARATION

• From the main fabric cut a piece the length of the central panel plus 7.5 cm (3 in), and the width of the central panel plus 3 cm (1¼ in).

• For the bottom border, cut a piece of ticking contrast A the depth of the border x two plus 3 cm (1¼ in) and the same width as the main fabric.

• For each side border, cut a piece of ticking contrast B as wide as the length of the side border plus 7.5 cm (3 in) (remember that the ticking stripe is on its side here), and as deep as the width of the border x two plus 3 cm (1¼ in).

• For the lining, cut a piece the same dimensions as the main fabric piece. Also from lining fabric, cut a single rod pocket to the same width plus 10 cm (4 in).

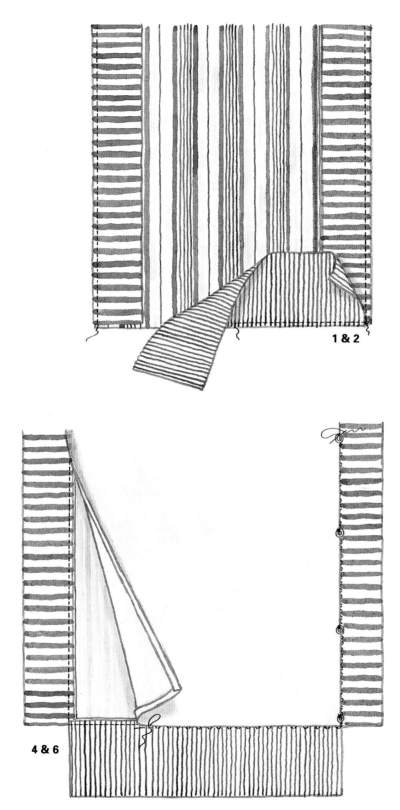

1 & 2

4 & 6

1 Take each side border piece and fold in half lengthways, with the rights sides together. Taking a 1.5 cm (⅝ in) seam allowance, stitch the bottom end of each of the borders closed. Turn the pieces of fabric right sides out and press. Now pin both of the side borders to the sides of the central panel, aligning raw edges and leaving 1.5 cm (⅝ in) at the bottom of the central panel free.

2 Take the bottom border piece and fold in half lengthways, with the right sides together. Taking a 1.5 cm (⅝ in) seam allowance, stitch up both ends of the folded fabric. Turn the fabric right side out, press, and then pin it to the bottom of the central panel, aligning raw edges and making sure that it meets the side borders at each of the bottom corners of the blind.

3 Starting at one top corner, stitch around three sides of the blind with a 1.5 cm (⅝ in) seam allowance, so that all three borders are attached. Press in all the seams towards the central panel.

4 With wrong sides facing, lay the lining onto the blind, aligning the top edges. Turn in a 1.5 cm (⅝ in) hem around the sides and bottom, and slipstitch the lining to the blind.

5 Measuring up from the bottom of the bottom border, mark the finished length of the blind along the top with pins. Fold over the top of the blind along this pinned line, press and trim back the raw edges to within 2 cm (¾ in). Remove the pins and attach the soft side of the Velcro strip with two rows of machine stitching.

6 Mark the positions of the brass rings in pencil on either side of the lining. Start with one on each bottom corner of the

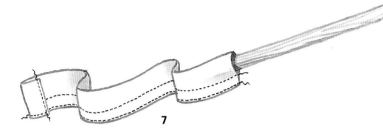

7

lining and leave 30 cm (12 in) between each ring. The last ring should fall approximately 30 cm (12 in) from the top of the blind. You can make your pleats shallower if, for instance, your window is quite small and you still want several pleats in your blind. To do this, simply reduce the distance between your rings. Sew on the hollow brass rings by hand through all layers of the blind making sure that they are very securely attached.

7 Make up a rod pocket as described in step 1 on page 54 and shown above. Insert the dowelling rod into the pocket and fold the open end of the pocket over twice and machine closed. Attach each end of the rod to the blind at the bottom of the lining with secure hand stitches.

8 Cut, cover and fix the batten as described in steps 7 and 8 on page 55.

9 String up the blind and check that it is pulling up level as described in steps 9 and 10 on page 55.

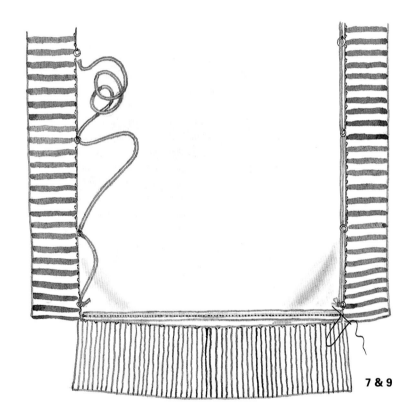

7 & 9

checks and stripes

checks and stripes

'There is a small mill in Lancashire that is like a living museum with looms that are more than 75 years old, that makes very traditional fabrics like shirtings for Jermyn Street and blanket check for horse blankets. While I was there, I spotted a roll of cream flannelette with a red stripe through it that I recognized from my National Service days as a cloth that was cut into squares and used to clean the barrel of a rifle. I persuaded them to make it as a check as well and we called it Rifle check and stripe.'

The Ian Mankin style is based on natural fabrics with only woven, as opposed to printed, designs. This means that, apart from the richly patterned (but still woven) Jacquard florals, the look is restricted to plains, stripes, checks and plaids. Given these limitations, it is surprising what a wealth of different fabrics are produced and just how many ways there are of putting them together. We have already looked at tickings as they warranted a chapter in their own right (see pages 56-69). Now it seems appropriate to take a closer look at traditional checks.

Gingham, all too familiar to anyone who ever wore it made up into shirts and dresses as summer school uniform, comes from the Malay word 'gingan'. It is an all-cotton, checked cloth made with equal numbers of dyed and undyed threads in the warp and weft, and usually with a double thread edging each check to give the raised effect of a dimity. Another word for gingham was zephyrs.

Now made in China, it is a fine fabric not usually thought of as a furnishing fabric. However, gingham looks homely as unlined curtains in a cottage kitchen or a child's bedroom, and as tablecloths and bed linen. It is also useful to use for borders and piping, and looks particularly good cut on the cross.

Another familiar check pattern is Madras. Named after a city on the south-east coast of India with a highly developed textile industry producing a wide variety of cloths, the name has long been synonymous with a fine, plain woven cotton plaid fabric. Again, it is a fabric familiar to many as the plaid shirts common in the sixties that ruined many a wash load because one of its characteristics is that the dyes bleed! Like gingham, it is a fine woven cotton not normally associated with furnishing fabrics. But used unlined as soft curtains or made up into striking bed linen, it is a cheerful addition to a room.

The Indian gift for subtle colour combinations have led them to carry on the tradition of Madras plaids on heavier furnishing-weight fabrics such as Masook. Sometimes they almost imitate a traditional Scottish tartan; with others, they create new and unusual plaids that can be used to striking effect in modern interiors. Plaids are enormously useful in a decorating scheme for pulling together disparate colours in a room. There may only be the narrowest stripe in a multi-coloured plaid that matches, say, the particular wall colour you are trying to introduce to a scheme. But if the other colours match the upholstery of your sofa, or the print of your curtain fabric, you may find that using that plaid as cushions or a throw unites the various constituents.

To all these checks and plaids add the ticking, Century Stripe linen, canvas stripes, and a rich array of Indian stripes and you begin to get the full Ian Mankin picture. Unifying them in a single decorating scheme requires a clear eye for colour and a bit of daring.

USING CHECKS AND STRIPES

To enliven a neutral living room, you could make up covers for scatter cushions in an array of checks and stripes and pile them onto a plain sofa. Or edge plain cushion covers with wide, bias-cut checked or striped borders, and tie them in with a similar border down the leading edge of a pair of curtains. If you are thinking of fas-

RED AND WHITE GINGHAM GIVES A HOMELY TOUCH TO A SWEDISH STYLED BEDROOM. THE TAUPE BACKGROUND OF THE RED STRIPED TICKING ON THE PILLOWCASES TIES IN WITH THE COLOUR ON THE WALLS.

tening your cushions in unusual ways, try making a tied closing on a checked cushion with striped ties, or a buttoned flap on a striped cushion in a check. Finally, use checks and stripes in endless combinations for patchwork and appliquéd cushions.

It is not hard to think of ways of using both checks and stripes together in a bedroom. Quilt covers and pillowcases offer lots of possibilities. Since you have to join together more than one width of fabric to make a piece wide enough for a quilt cover, why not think of the extra width in terms of wide borders so that, for instance, you edge the checked central panel of your cover with striped borders and then carry the idea through to the pillowcases as well? If you don't want to be bothered with making all the bed linen from scratch, customize an existing set of striped or plain linen with bias-cut checked borders. Tie them in with a new pair of curtains in the same check and perhaps a bed valance, and you will have given your bedroom an entirely new look.

Take your imagination on into the kitchen and you can achieve a country kitchen atmosphere combining checks and stripes. Use unlined gingham to curtain off the cupboards beneath your work surfaces, perhaps using a sturdier, contrasting ticking to make the heading punched with brass eyelets slotted onto narrow brass rods. Then carry that idea through to café curtains at the windows and ticking squab cushions with gingham piping for your kitchen chairs.

A WARM AND INVITING DINING ROOM WHERE THE SEAT CUSHIONS, THE CHECKED CURTAINS AND THE PLAID SCATTER CUSHIONS ON THE CHAISE LONGUE WORK VERY WELL TOGETHER. NOTE HOW THE RED STRIPE IN THE PLAID HELPS TO UNITE THE OTHER COLOURS WITH THE RED OF THE PAINTED FURNITURE.

MAKING A CHECK AND STRIPE ORGANIZER

You can purchase canvas wardrobe organizers like the one featured opposite in sizes to accommodate sweaters or shoes, and decorated with simple appliquéd motifs like this, they can come out of the closet and be used for children's toys, clothes or even books.

The motifs are stuck onto the sides of the organizer with a double-sided, iron-on fixative, which comes in sheets sold by the metre (yard) and has waxed paper stuck to one side. Trace the motifs onto the paper side of the fixative and then follow step 4 on page 82 for attaching it to the organizer. Repeat the process with details on the motifs, such as the bird's wing, using contrasting fabric.

When you have applied motifs down both sides of the organizer it only remains to add some pretty tapes to the top to tie it to a pole straddling the corner of a room. There are other places in the house, apart from a child's room, where an organizer like this could prove useful – in a hall for gloves, scarves and hats, for example, or in the corner of the kitchen for tea towels and table linen.

CHECKS AND STRIPES – THE PRACTICALITIES

• Don't be afraid to cover a large piece of furniture such as a sofa in a bold plaid. Care must be taken, however, to match the checks. On some plaids, especially on hand-woven fabrics, this can be practically impossible and one way of minimizing the number of joins is to make seat cushions where the top and bottom are cut in one continuous piece with the front stand.

• The problem of matching hand-woven checks and plaids also means that they are not a good choice of fabric to use for Roman blinds. The flat expanse of fabric, which then has to pleat up very evenly, draws attention to any unevenness in the plaid. If you really want to use a plaid or check on a Roman or roller blind, limit it to a border, either down the sides, or simply a deep one across the bottom.

• On curtains that are gathered, matching a check is not quite so crucial. As long as the checks meet and run as horizontally as possible near the top of the curtain, the eye will not notice if the checks do not match perfectly lower down among the folds of cloth.

opposite A BOUGHT ORGANIZER CAN BE CHARMINGLY TRANSFORMED WITH BOLD, BRIGHT APPLIQUE PICTURES.

overleaf CHECKED AND STRIPED FABRICS COMBINE SO NATURALLY. THE BRIGHT COLOURS CHOSEN FOR THIS CHILD'S ROOM MAKE IT BOTH CHEERFUL AND PLAYFUL.

child's quilt

PREPARATION

- Work out your design on squared paper or, if you want to make one exactly like this, use the following cutting list:

- Devon Check: 2 pieces, each measuring 33 x 89 cm (13 x 35 in)

- Ticking 2 peony: 1 piece measuring 23 x 93 cm (9 x 40 in)
- Ticking 2 airforce: 1 piece measuring 33 x 93 cm (13 x 40 in)
- Ticking 1: 2 pieces, each measuring 18 x 89 cm (7 x 35 in)

- 6 mm (¼ in) gingham: 1 piece measuring 8 x 93 cm (3 x 40 in)
- 3 mm (⅛ in) gingham: 1 length of bias-cut strip in each colour, each measuring 2.5 m long x 13 cm wide (2¾ yd long x 5 in wide).

YOU WILL NEED

- 0.5 M (20 IN) EACH OF DEVON CHECK IN PEONY AND NAVY

- 0.3 M (12 IN) EACH OF TICKING 2 IN PEONY AND AIRFORCE

- 0.2 M (8 IN) EACH OF TICKING 1 IN PEONY AND AIRFORCE

- 0.1 M (4 IN) OF 6 MM (¼ IN) GINGHAM IN BLUE

- 1 M (1 YD) EACH OF 3 MM (⅛ IN) GINGHAM IN RED AND BLUE

- 2OZ POLYESTER WADDING – SINGLE BEDSPREAD SIZE

- SPRAY GLUE

- 1.5 M (60 IN) OF CLUB STRIPE IN NAVY

- SCRAPS OF RED AND BLUE FABRICS

- BONDAWEB

- RED AND BLUE BUTTONS

1

1 Sew all the pieces together as the patchwork illustrated on page 80, taking 1.5 cm (⅝ in) seam allowances and pressing seams open as you go. Sew together the bias strips of gingham and stitch around the edge of the patchwork, being careful not to stretch the bias. Turn in the border 1.5 cm (⅝ in) along its raw edge, and then again 5 cm (2 in).

2 Cut the polyester wadding to fit the patchwork. Lay the patchwork face down on a flat surface, making sure it is well pressed and that there are no wrinkles. Lay the wadding on top. Wearing a mask and making sure the room is well ventilated, fold back half of the wadding and spray glue onto the back of the patchwork, and then lay the wadding back down. Fold back the other half of the wadding and repeat the operation.

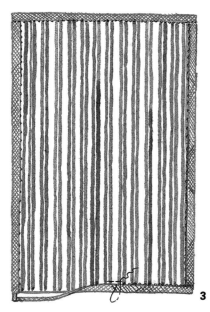

3 Cut a piece of Club Stripe to the same size as the wadding and lay that in place on top of the wadding, wrong side down. Fold the gingham binding over the top of the Club Stripe and slip stitch in place.

4 Using the outlines right and below, draw or trace your appliqué motifs onto the paper side of the Bondaweb and cut them out roughly. Iron onto the wrong side of the assorted fabric scraps and cut them out precisely. Peel off the paper backing and place them in position on the patchwork. Press with a damp cloth for at least 15 seconds on a moderate setting, making sure that you cover all parts of the motif with the iron. It is important that you follow these instructions so that all the adhesive has time to bond, making the appliqué dry-cleanable.

5 Sew buttons onto the appliqués, through all layers of the quilt.

nursery curtains

These simple curtains are made almost totally by machine. They are lined with a contrast fabric rather than a plain lining so it is important to choose a fabric which will not fade drastically when exposed to direct sunlight. The English woven ticking that has been used here is ideal for this purpose. To work out how much fabric you will need, see Measuring up on pages 120-1. To your finished drop measurement add 30 cm (12 in) for the flap at the top of the curtain, and 10 cm (4 in) for the hem.

When you hang your curtains, allow the top edge of the curtain to flop forwards, and loop back the curtains to a hook set into the window frame at a height that will reveal the right amount of ticking.

YOU WILL NEED

- MAIN FABRIC IN DEVON CHECK

- LINING IN TICKING 2

- LEAD PENNY WEIGHTS

- 3 MM (⅛ IN) GINGHAM IN NAVY AS BINDING

- CHALK

- RULER

- 8 CM (3 IN) WIDE PENCIL PLEAT HEADING TAPE

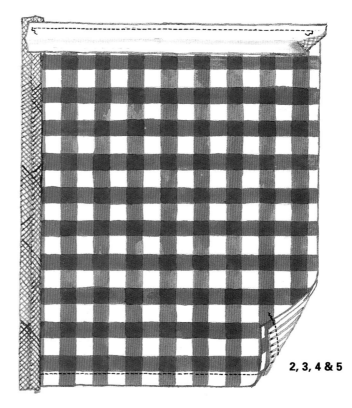

2, 3, 4 & 5

1 Cut enough 3 mm (⅛ in) gingham into 8 cm (3 in) wide bias strips to bind three sides of each curtain. Sew the strips together (see page 119) to make enough of a continuous length to bind each curtain. Cut the Devon Check into the required lengths and as it is wider than the ticking, cut it down to the same width. Cut the ticking into the lengths required less 3 cm (1¼ in). If you are using more than one width per curtain, sew your widths together with right sides facing and press open the seams.

2 Press up a 5 cm (2 in) double hem along the bottom of the Devon Check and tack a covered lead penny weight (see page 122) into the hem at least 3 cm

(1¼ in) in from the either end, and also at the bottom of each seam if you have more than one drop. Machine the hem.

3 Press up a 4 cm (1½ in) double hem in the ticking and machine. With wrong sides together, spread the two fabrics flat with the top edges and sides aligned and the hem of the ticking 1 cm (½ in) shorter than the check. Pin together.

4 Press the bias strip in half lengthways, wrong sides together. Starting at the bottom corner of one side of the curtain with the Devon Check face up, lay one raw edge of the bias strip along the side of the curtain (leaving a 2 cm [¾ in] overhang, for turning in later), and machine sew through all three layers taking a 2 cm (¾ in) seam allowance. Take care not to stretch the bias strip too much as you go. When you get to the top of the curtain, cut your bias strip, again leaving a 2 cm (¾ in) overhang.

5 Repeat the process along the top of the curtain and again down the other side.

6 From the check side of the curtain, press the bias strip over towards the

7 & 8

outside edge of the curtain. Turn the curtain over to the stripe side and then press over the raw edge of the binding so that the raw edges are enclosed in the 2 cm (¾ in) wide gingham binding. Slip stitch all the way around the inside edge of the binding, turning in and neatening the corners as you go.

7 With the ticking side of the curtain still uppermost, measure 30 cm (12 in) down from the top edge and draw a chalk line all the way across the curtain. Using this line as a guide, machine the top edge of the pencil pleat tape across the width of the curtain.

8 Using some left-over bias-cut strip, make two loops about 5 cm (2 in) long and tuck the ends into the hand-sewn side of the binding on the leading edge of each curtain 20 cm (8 in) up from the hem. Hand sew securely in place.

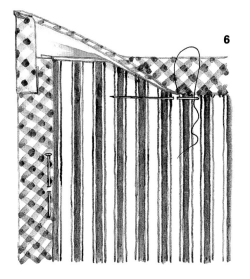

6

headboard cover

PREPARATION

- Make a template by tracing the shape of the headboard onto paper. Depending on the thickness of the headboard add an ease allowance all around the sides and top of the shape you have traced. In this particular case, the headboard was made of cane and 2.5 cm (1 in) was added, but if yours is quite thickly padded, you may want to add a little more.

- Add a 1.5 cm (⅝ in) seam allowance all around the sides and top of the shape, and a 5 cm (2 in) hem allowance to the bottom edge.

- Transfer this shape twice onto the Masook and cut them out.

- Join the 8cm (3in) wide bias-cut fabric into long strips (see page 119).

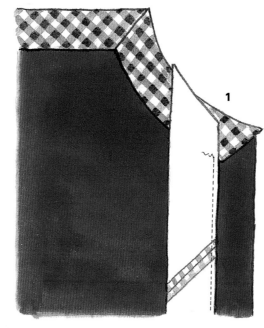

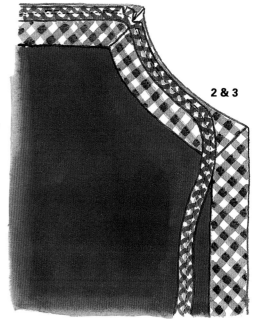

1 Draw a chalk line onto the front piece of Masook 6.5 cm (2½ in) from the edge. Stitch the wider bias-cut gingham along this line, leaving a 1.5 cm (⅝ in) seam allowance to the right of the stitch line. If your headboard is shaped, back stitch where the shape starts; cut the gingham strip, leaving a generous amount to fold in.

2 For each subsequent run of shape, start stitching again with another piece of gingham strip from exactly the same spot where you finished off before. Press the border towards the outer edge, folding the corners into neat mitres (see page 122). Cut away any excess fabric, and hand sew the mitres.

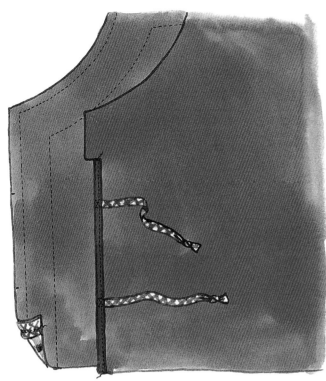

4, 5 & 6

7

3 Make up the narrower bias-cut gingham into enough piping to run along three sides of the headboard (see pages 118-119). Using a piping foot, stitch the piping 1.5 cm (⅝ in) in around three sides of the headboard shape.

4 The sides of the headboard cover are left open for ease of removal and held closed with narrow ties. Decide on the point from which the side seams should be left open, perhaps about 10 cm (4 in) down from the top of the side seam, and clip into the seam allowance of the front and back piece at this point.

5 Now decide on the position of the ties on the headboard and mark the position onto the front and back pieces. Make eight narrow ties about 20 cm (8 in) long by folding the remains of the narrower

bias-cut strips in half lengthways and stitching 1 cm (½ in) in from the fold line. Use a safety pin to turn each tie right side out and finish one end of the tie by tying a knot in it.

6 On the back piece, fold in a 1 cm (½ in) double hem down the open sides and to the wrong side of the fabric from the point where you have clipped into the seam allowance downwards. Tuck the ties into the hem where they have been marked and stitch down the side hems, back stitching over the ties to make sure they are securely anchored. Do the same on the other side.

7 For the front, cut two plackets of Masook 8 cm (3 in) wide by the length of the side openings. Turn in a 1 cm (½ in) double hem along one long edge of both these pieces. Pin the ties to the front piece where their positions have been marked. Then lay a placket face down onto the right side of the front piece with the raw edge of the placket along the side opening of the front piece. Using a piping foot, machine stitch the placket to the front piece, back stitching securely over the ties.

8 Make up a pocket piece big enough to carry a child's book or toy. Cut out the fabric to your desired shape and size and then decorate it by adding a border and an appliquéd animal using Bondaweb (see step 4 in the Child's quilt on page 82). Turn in a 1 cm (½ in) hem around three sides of the pocket and stitch into position towards one side on the front of the cover. Don't centre the pocket to the

height of the fabric as the finished cover will be tucked in behind the mattress and pillows. Instead, position it towards the top of the headboard, as in the photograph on page 89.

9 Lay the back and front pieces right sides together and, using a piping foot, sew them together from the point where you have clipped into the seam allowance on one side, up and across the top to the point where you have clipped on the other side.

10 Fold up a 2.5 cm (1 in) double hem along the bottom edge of both the front and back and stitch. Finally, turn the headboard cover right sides out, slip it over the headboard and then make the ties into little bows.

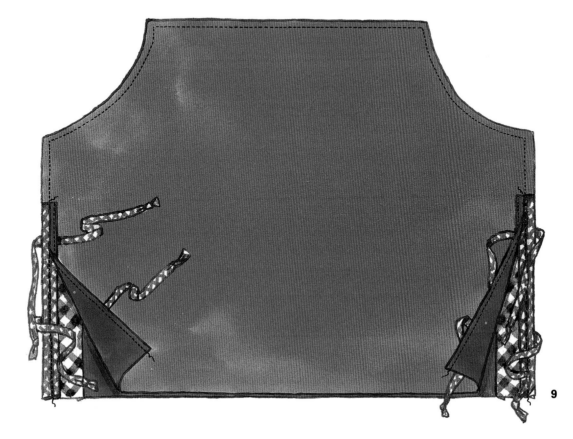

9

jacquard

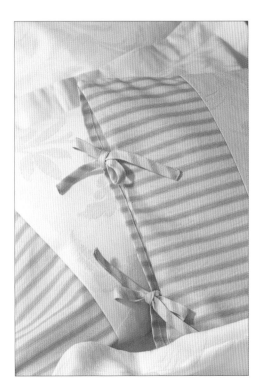

jacquard

A JACQUARD LOOM, NAMED
AFTER ITS INVENTOR JOSEPH
MARIE JACQUARD.

'Some years ago, I gave a brief talk to a group of decorators in San Francisco. I opened with the sentence, "I have to be honest with you all and confess that I know very little about textiles." A good case in point is Jacquards – to this day I don't understand the complexities of the Jacquard loom, but we are working on a new range of designs now. The art I collect is often very simple line drawings. I'm trying to reproduce that very graphic style in textiles, in a Jacquard, with natural kinds of images. I think it's going to work.'

Jacquard is the term for a shedding mechanism attached to a loom that enables large and elaborate designs to be woven. A series of perforated cards gives individual control of hundreds of warp threads, regulating which are lifted and which are lowered to form the design.

Before the invention of the Jacquard loom, textiles with a complicated pattern such as damasks and brocades were woven on a drawloom. This relatively primitive machine relied on the presence of a small child to crawl around underneath the loom as the shuttle shot backwards and forwards, lifting and lowering by hand the necessary warp threads that formed the pattern.

Joseph Marie Jacquard was born the son of a weaver in 1752 in Lyon in France, and throughout his childhood was a *tireur-de-lac*, as the child labourers were called. This formative experience was, not surprisingly, enough to put him off weaving, and he opted for an apprenticeship in book binding. The move brought him into contact with technology and machines somewhat more advanced than the drawlooms from which he had escaped driving him to spend many years trying to adapt this technology to the weaving process.

In 1801, Joseph Marie unveiled his Jacquard loom at the Paris Exhibition where it won an award. But it was not until 1804, when he had ironed out some of the loom's initial flaws, that the mechanism that we know today began to come into commercial use. By the 1820s, the Jacquard loom was in widespread use throughout the weaving centres of Europe. While child labour was by no means dispensed with in the mills over the next century, this development was no doubt one step towards a more humane age.

A PRETTY ROLLER BLIND, TRIMMED WITH A SCALLOPED TICKING BORDER, LETS THE SUNSHINE THROUGH THE RICHLY FLORAL PATTERNED JACQUARD.

A Jacquard loom is used to weave damask. The term damask refers to its origins in Damascus in Syria, and describes a patterned cloth, familiar to all as that commonly used for tablecloths. The sheen of the design runs in the opposite direction from that in the background so that the design stands out very clearly, despite being woven in one colour only. Most of the Jacquards stocked in the Ian Mankin shops are damask.

Since the original concept for Ian Mankin's shop was to stock only woven plains, stripes and checks, it was fitting that the first Jacquard design he commissioned was a copy of one of the ticking stripes. It is probably true to say that his innovation was that he sold it loomstate, or in its natural, unbleached state, before the cloth is scoured to remove the cotton seeds, and dyed. If you lay a dyed cream damask next to a natural Ian Mankin Jacquard, you will see that despite initially appearing to be similar in colour there is, in fact, little comparison. The dyed fabric will look lifeless, uniform and flat.

Following on from those early stripes, the next step of allowing a richly floral fabric through the hallowed portals of his linear world seemed daring. However, 'Thistle', the name Ian Mankin gave to what was, in fact, a very traditional damask design but which again he sold in loom-

state, proved one of his most popular fabrics. It was followed by the even more naturalistic floral designs of 'Springflower' and 'Wildflower', and these are hopefully to be superseded by a new range depicting fruits and vegetables.

USING JACQUARD

The rich patterned sheen of Jacquard lends itself to thickly interlined curtains. Gather them generously with a narrow gathering tape set down some way from the top of the curtain so that it forms a deep frill above the tape. You can plump out the frill with more interlining and then softly shape it with randomly placed stab stitches to form a puffed heading that falls down in front of the tape. This heading will only really work if the curtains are not drawn but are left as a fixed heading and swept back with, say, an opulent tasselled rope tieback.

If you are trying to create a more formal look, make up Jacquard as curtains with deep swags and tails, lined perhaps with a contrast colour or even a check which will show where the tails fold back. Or gather the fullness of a pair of generous interlined curtains with heavy goblet pleats and sew buttons covered in a tiny check at the base of each pleat.

Since Jacquard or, strictly speaking, damask is traditionally used for table linen, it is a natural choice for a dining room. Create an elegant, candle-lit atmosphere with heavily swagged curtains and a tablecloth that reaches to the floor with a deep bullion fringe around the hem. Since this will not be easily laundered, it should be an undercloth, with another, smaller, cloth made with neatly turned hems to go on top.

AS A FINISHING TOUCH, MAKE A SIMPLE DRAWSTRING COVER FOR A HOT-WATER BOTTLE FROM A STRIPED SATIN JACQUARD.

The richly patterned but neutral colour of natural Jacquard makes a good backdrop to show off opulent trimmings such as ropes and fringes, tassels and braids. There is an increasingly wide array available nowadays, from historically accurate reproductions of extravagant passementerie to simpler versions made in natural materials such as linen and sisal. Curtain trimmings are hardly ever cheap since they are usually laboriously hand-made, but if used with restraint, they can make a stunning addition to an interior.

So, trim your swags and tails with a tasselled fringe. Link goblet pleats with a rope twisted into a knot at the base of each pleat, ending in a long drop of rope at each end of the heading finished with a silky tassel. Trim the leading edge of an interlined Jacquard curtain with a thick but short fringe in a deeply contrasting colour, or use the same fringe to edge velvet cushions to pile on a Jacquard covered sofa for a richly textured look.

If you are very adept with a sewing machine, it is possible to quilt Jacquard by bonding the fabric to a thin layer of polyester wadding and then following the outline of the design with machine stitching. Use it quilted to make a simple tie-on cover for a bedhead. Or quilt a rectangle and hang it from a curtain pole with café clips as an unstructured pelmet, where the curtains hang from a track hidden behind it. Or quilt just one large flower and make it up into a small cushion, to nestle among others on a bed or sofa.

However, to emphasize the large, elaborate patterns on Jacquard, it is best to treat it very simply. Unlined Roman blinds or roller blinds look marvellous when the sun shines through them, projecting the pattern into glorious sharp relief. Or make unlined Jacquard curtains with hardly any fullness, with a flat heading using sew-on hooks to hang them from a narrow metal pole. When drawn, they make a softly hanging screen across the window, allowing the pattern to shine through when backlit by daylight.

JACQUARD – THE PRACTICALITIES

• Jacquard is made from 100 per cent cotton, and will shrink slightly when washed. So if you are planning to make it into something that is to be washed rather than dry-cleaned, make allowances for shrinkage in your measurements, or wash it before making up. The pattern raises slightly when washed, which is a pleasing effect.

• When you are using the large floral patterns on Jacquard for curtains, take account of the pattern repeat when estimating fabric quantities (see estimating fabric for curtains on page 121).

overleaf JACQUARD AND TICKING COMBINE TO MAKE BEAUTIFULLY LARGE PILLOWCASES TO PILE HIGH ON A BED.

jacquard pillowcase

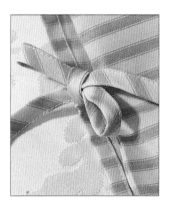

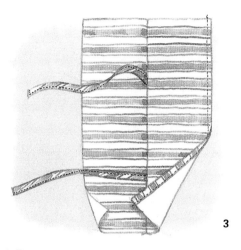

1 For the ties, take each of the bias strips and turn in a narrow hem on three sides. Then press the whole strip in half lengthways with wrong sides together and stitch close to the edge.

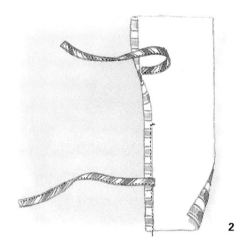

2

YOU WILL NEED

- 4 PIECES OF BIAS STRIPS, EACH MEASURING **4 x 25 CM (1½ x 10 IN)**

- 3 PIECES OF TICKING STRIPE, EACH MEASURING **18 x 53 CM (7 x 21 IN)**

- 1 PIECE OF JACQUARD SPRINGFLOWER MEASURING **123 x 53 CM (48½ x 21 IN)**

2 Take one piece of ticking and turn in a 5 mm (¼ in) hem on one long edge. Then turn in again by 1 cm (½ in) and tuck in the end of a tie, 14 cm (5½ in) from each side. Stitch along hem, ensuring the ties are secure by back stitching several times.

3

3 Take the other two pieces of ticking and lay them right sides together. Position the remaining ties 14 cm (5½ in) in from each side and stitch a 1.5 cm (⅝ in) seam, securely anchoring the ties by back stitching several times. Press the seam open. Neaten one long edge by pressing a 5 mm (¼ in) hem and then a 1 cm (½ in) hem, stitching close to the inside fold.

4 With right sides together and raw edges aligned, sew the single piece of ticking to one end of the Jacquard. Sew the double piece of ticking to the other end of the Jacquard. Press the seams open.

5 Lay the strip right side up on your worksurface. Take the single piece of ticking end and fold it over until the seam lies on top of the ticking/Jacquard seam at the other end. Fold the double piece of ticking back over the top so that its neatened edge lies against the seams.

6 Stitch along both side seams taking 1.5 cm (⅝ in) seam allowances and securely back stitch at each end. Turn the pillowcase right sides out and press.

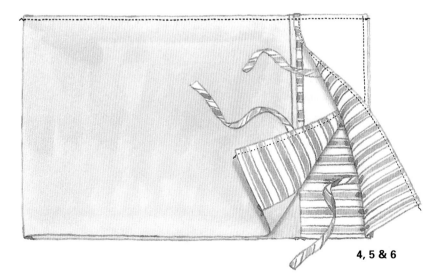

4, 5 & 6

pleated dressing table top

We found a delightful old pine desk with a kidney-shaped top and made a cover from a piece of Jacquard with a floral design incorporated into the weave to turn it into a pretty dressing table. To finish it off, the shelves beneath have been lined with scraps of ticking.

YOU WILL NEED

1 M (1 YD) JACQUARD
SPRINGFLOWER

1 M (1 YD) TICKING 2

PIPING CORD

DOUBLE-SIDED TAPE

1 Make a template of the top of the table out of newspaper and add 2 cm (¾ in) seam allowance all the way around. Use the template to cut out the Jacquard.

2 Cut enough 5 cm (2 in)-wide bias cut strips out of the ticking to go around the edge of the table. Make up piping (see page 118) and stitch it to the Jacquard, leaving a 1.5 cm (⅝ in) seam allowance.

3 Measure all the way around the edge of the table top and multiply the measurement by one-and-a-half. Cut strips of Jacquard, 13 cm (5 in) deep x this measurement. Sew the strips together into a ring, press open the seams, and turn up a 5 mm (¼ in) hem and then a 1 cm (½ in) hem all around the bottom edge and hand stitch.

4 With right sides together, pin the frill to the table top, distributing the fullness evenly all the way around. Start to machine on the frill with a piping foot, taking up the fullness in little tucks every 5 cm (2 in) (with a bit of practice you should be able to do this by eye). Press all the seam allowances towards the frill.

5 Put the cover onto the table top, and secure it with double-sided tape around the edge. Cut pieces of ticking the size of the shelves plus 1 cm (½ in) all around. Press in the 1 cm (½ in) allowances. Stick a grid of double-sided tape onto the shelves, and carefully position the ticking.

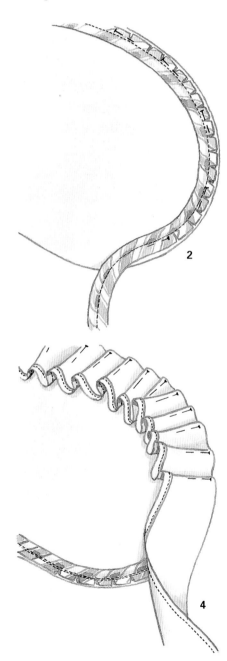

muslin

muslin

MUSLIN, IN ITS MOST BASIC
LOOMSTATE, HAS MANY CULINARY
PURPOSES. HERE IT IS USED TO
WRAP THE CURD FOR CREAM
CHEESE, SO THAT IT CAN BE HUNG
AND LEFT TO DRAIN OVERNIGHT.

'I was travelling on holiday on a train to the South of France with my wife and children and we got into conversation with a fellow traveller. It transpired that he was a textile merchant from Manchester and for fifty years his family business, Btesh Brothers, had been involved in exporting a very fine Egyptian cotton muslin exclusively to the Middle East. But the market had suddenly dried up because of competition from the Far East. Some time later, when I opened the shop, I contacted him again. He had over 20,000 yards in stock in his warehouse and in the end we sold the lot.'

Some say that the word muslin derives from Mosul, an area in Iraq; others from the Hindi word 'mulmull' which has been used in India for three centuries to describe a plain woven, fine, sheer and soft cotton cloth.

Butter muslin, cheesecloth, mutton cloth, mull, gauze and flag bunting are all from the muslin family. The first three of these names refer specifically to their intended culinary purpose – the wrappings for butter, cheeses, bacon, meat and even plum puddings. Butter muslin is still used today for such purposes and for straining and clarifying soups and sauces, and these practical origins are reflected in its coarse nature. In its unbleached state, butter muslin retains the small dark flecks of the cotton seed which are removed in further refining and bleaching processes. However, in an age where we crave the simple and the natural, these humble flaws add a certain charm.

In contrast, as long ago as the seventeenth century, in Dacca (now part of Bangladesh), craftsmen were spinning and weaving cotton entirely by hand into the most extraordinarily fine cloth which was used only for royal and ceremonial occasions. Dacca muslin was so light that 66 m (72 yd) weighed only 450 g (1 lb), or less than a quarter of the weight of a fine quality muslin today. At the Great Exhibition in Hyde Park in 1851, Victorian Britain came to admire, among other things, the fine crafts from each of her colonies. Of all the exotic cloths from the

Indian sub-continent, it was the hand-woven muslin from Dacca that caused a stir. As fine as a cobweb, with dainty 'butis', or floral sprigs, embroidered in a thicker yarn, that it could possibly have been made by hand was considered a marvel, even in those days.

Nowadays, the finest 'silky' muslin is not made from silk at all, but from the best Egyptian cotton. Egyptian cotton, the name of which no longer refers only to its country of origin, is a type of cotton plant that produces one of the highest quality cottons in the world. It is the length and quality, or staple, of the cotton fibre which governs how fine a yarn can be spun. Except perhaps for Sea Island cotton from the USA, Egyptian cotton has the longest and finest staple and this explains why muslin woven from its yarn is so exquisitely light and delicate with a subtle lustre that even extends to the selvedge.

In the past, muslin was used for 'casement' or 'glass' cloths – lightweight curtains that were hung close to the glass. However, during the Napoleonic Empire period of decoration in France at the turn of the nineteenth century, muslin was used in lavish curtain arrangements, swagged over arrow-headed brass rods, trimmed with lace and beading, and hung with swathes of rich fabrics such as satin and velvet. During the same period in Germany, the less ostentatious muslin curtains complemented the simpler style of Biedermeier.

Unfortunately, in more recent times, the advent of synthetic materials have given net curtains a bad name. While nylon seems to offer labour saving, 'easy care' advantages, more often than not nylon net curtains look grey and mean

MUSLIN IS SO INEXPENSIVE IT MAKES A PRETTY ALTERNATIVE TO WRAPPING PAPER AND HAS BEEN USED TO FESTIVE EFFECT HERE TO WRAP THE TUB FOR THE CHRISTMAS TREE.

and have become synonymous with suburban nosiness. It is little wonder that today there is a recognized return to the use of natural cotton muslin to screen windows from busy streets outside, or ugly views, or to filter strong sunlight and soften the lines of a modern interior.

USING MUSLIN

As a natural alternative to the ubiquitous nylon net, slot cotton muslin generously onto net rods, with a stand above the slot to form a pretty frill. You can also make a slot at the hem for another rod to create the fixed curtains one sees so often in France on the inside of casement windows or glass doors (although it is important that the muslin is fully shrunk before you start). Or for a Japanese effect, make a flat banner of muslin with a slot at top and bottom. Hang it from a net rod fixed inside the inner frame of a window so that it is just covering the glass and reveals the woodwork. Hide another rod, that is not fixed, in the bottom slot for weight.

You can make blinds out of muslin, too. Roller blinds are difficult because the fabric distorts when stiffened, but Roman blinds that pleat up horizontally are effective. Make up the rod pockets as one with the blind, and use heavier fabric as borders to hide the cord mechanism and add stability and weight. An interesting idea for a window with an ugly view is to make a blind where the top half is made from muslin to let in light, while the bottom half is made of an opaque fabric to screen out the view.

For outer curtains, you can slot muslin generously onto a thick wooden pole, with a frill above, perhaps 7.5 cm (3 in) deep, caught back with rope tiebacks; and so you don't have to interfere with your muslin arrangement, use a roller blind behind it for privacy. Exploit the transparency of muslin by layering stripes over plain, sweeping the top layer aside with rope or a metal holdback. Use its filmy lightweight qualities to the full by swagging it casually over poles or bed frames.

Trimmings such as braid, fringe or ribbon can be used for practical as well as decorative reasons – they can help to finish the edges neatly and add weight. Borders of a heavier-weight contrast fabric can be used in the same way, either along the leading edge as a finish, or deeply across the hem to add weight. Another way to finish the edges is simply to fray them, although this would be a laborious task on anything other than relatively small stretches.

Above all, remember that muslin, particularly butter muslin, is cheap so you can afford to be generous, temporary and frivolous – forget your needle and

opposite SOFT WHITE MUSLIN IS DRAPED OVER A POLE AT THE WINDOW AND FROM HIGH ABOVE A SLEIGH BED TO CREATE A FAIRY TALE SETTING.

thread and tack it up with a staple gun, or simply tie it into place. Tent a ceiling instead of re-decorating. Swathe a bed for romance. Swag a table for a celebration. Dipped into a solution of flour and water, you can arrange strips of muslin into bows and bake them in a very low oven to make stiff decorative bows, sprayed with silver and gold for Christmas.

You can dye muslin very easily as cotton is extremely receptive to dyes – navy blue, vermilion, cerise or way-out orange make a strong statement. And you can use fabric paints or crayons, stencils or stamps to create you own designs – gold stars on coarse, unbleached butter muslin look wonderful, and for white on white calligraphy you don't even need to be able to draw.

MUSLIN – THE PRACTICALITIES

• All cotton muslin will shrink. Allowances of up to 10 per cent must be added to your calculations when estimating how much cloth you will need. Strictly, it is then necessary to wash the fabric before use but this is a laborious task (especially ironing it afterwards) and you will lose some of that 'brand new' quality, so wherever possible simply make your lengths 10 per cent too long, let them cascade on the floor and wait until the first clean is absolutely necessary to shrink them.

• It is best to be generous when using muslin, particularly the silky variety which is so fine it will gather up to nothing and has a tendency to crinkle itself into 'Fortuny pleats'. This can be a pleasing effect but may not cover the area originally intended. Three or four times the width should be used.

• When making curtains with several widths of muslin, it is best not to sew the lengths together down the side seams – it is difficult to do this without puckering and since the fabric is so transparent you won't be hiding anything. Instead, leave each length hanging individually. First, make sure each drop is cut to precisely the same length, then hem each drop and, if you are using curtain tape, sew it to the top of the first drop and then run it straight across onto the top of the next drop, overlapping the sides slightly as you go.

• After washing muslin, spray starch will make ironing it easier.

---

opposite FOR A FRESH AND AIRY BATHROOM, USE MUSLIN IN LARGE QUANTITIES. HERE IT HAS BEEN USED TO MAKE A ROMAN BLIND (SEE PAGES 114-16 FOR MAKING INSTRUCTIONS) AND A LIGHTWEIGHT SHOWER CURTAIN.

laundry bag

YOU WILL NEED

- 2 PIECES OF NET, EACH
MEASURING **63 x 88 CM**
(25 x 34½ IN)

- 1 PIECE OF ELLIOT PLAID
MEASURING **123 x 81.5 CM**
(48½ x 32 IN)

- 2 M (2 YD) LENGTH
OF CORD

- BUTTON

6

1 Lay the pieces of net together and taking a 1.5 cm (⅝ in) seam allowance, stitch down each side, leaving a 2.5 cm (1 in) gap 12.5 cm (5 in) from the top edge, and stopping 6 cm (2½ in) from the bottom. Leave the bottom end open, press open the seams and turn right sides out.

2 Fold the plaid in half lengthways, right sides facing. Taking a 1.5 cm (⅝ in) seam allowance, stitch the sides to make a bag. Press open the seams.

3 Put the net inside the plaid with the top ends together. Taking a 1.5 cm (⅝ in) seam allowance, stitch the bags together around the top.

4 Pull the net out of the plaid bag and fold over the outside of the plaid until the raw edges meet at the bottom. Sew those edges together with a 6 cm (2½ in) seam allowance. Fray up to that stitch line to make a fringe.

5 To make the cord channel, sew two rows of stitches around the bag above and below the openings in the net side seams. Cut the cord into two and use a safety pin to thread one length through one of the openings and through the cord channel until it comes out of the same opening. Remove the safety pin, knot together the two ends and fray the cord up to the knot. Repeat with the other cord, but from the other opening.

6 Make a hanging loop with a strip of the plaid measuring 7 x 31 cm (2¾ x 12 in). Fold in a 1 cm (½ in) hem along both sides, then fold in half lengthways and

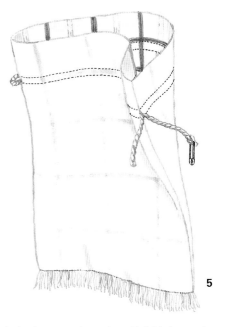

5

stitch close to the edge. Fold it into a loop and position on the bag, just above one of the cord openings, tucking the raw ends under. Machine a square of stitches with a cross through the middle to secure it.

7 Make a pocket out of plaid by cutting a piece about 30 x 18 cm (12 x 7 in). Fold in a 2.5 cm (1 in) double hem along one long edge and top stitch. Fold in a 1 cm (½ in) hem along the remaining sides and position on the bag front. Stitch it in place by sewing close to the edge around three sides of the pocket. Make a buttonhole in the pocket and sew on the button.

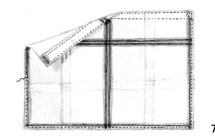

7

bathroom blind

This delicate, striped, muslin Roman blind is bordered all the way around with ticking stripe (see the picture on page 113) and, because it is unlined, the rod pockets are made by making pleats in the blind after the borders have been attached.

Measure your window (see pages 120-1) and decide how wide you wish the borders to be and how many rod pockets you will need. Here, the rod pockets are 20 cm (8 in) apart, after allowing for most of the bottom border to hang below the pleats.

• YOU WILL NEED

- STRIPED MUSLIN AND TICKING 2

- VELCRO (SEW AND STICK)

- HOLLOW BRASS RINGS (2 PER ROD POCKET)

- 9 MM (⅜ IN) DOWELLING RODS BY THE NUMBER OF POCKETS

- 5 X 2.5 CM (2 X 1 IN) SOFTWOOD BATTEN

- SAW

- HEAVY-DUTY STAPLE GUN

- 3 SCREW EYES

- TWO 4 CM (1½ IN) ANGLED BRACKETS

- ROMAN BLIND CORD

- SMALL BRASS CLEAT

- ACORN OR CORD WEIGHT

PREPARATION

- Cut the striped muslin to the width of your central panel plus 3 cm (1¼ in) seam allowance x the length of your central panel plus 5 cm (2 in) for each rod pocket plus 3 cm (1¼ in) seam allowance.

- Cut the ticking for the bottom border as wide as the central panel plus 3 cm (1¼ in) seam allowance by the depth of the border x 2 plus 3 cm (1¼ in).

- Cut the ticking for the top border as wide as the central panel plus 3 cm (1¼ in) by the depth of the border x 2 plus 3 cm (1¼ in).

- Cut the ticking for the side borders as wide as the overall length of the blind before the rod pockets are pleated plus 6.5 cm (2½ in) (you may have to cut two pieces and join them) by the width of the border x 2 plus 3 cm (1¼ in).

1 Cut out the muslin central panel and all the ticking border panels. If any of the border pieces need to be joined, join them now. Press all the border panels in half lengthways, wrong sides facing, and then open them out again.

2 With right sides together, machine the bottom border piece to the bottom edge of the muslin central panel. Press the seam allowances down towards the border, press in a 1.5 cm (⅝ in) turning along the bottom edge of the border, and then fold the whole border over to the back and slip stitch the folded edge of the border to the machine stitch line by hand.

3 Repeat step 2 for the top border.

4 Repeat step 2 for both the side borders covering the top and bottom borders to

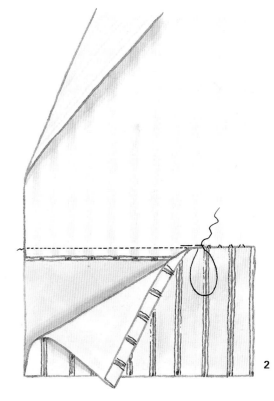

2

complete the rectangle. Fold in the 1.5 cm (⅝ in) seam allowance at the bottom corners and slip stitch.

5 Now lay out the blind on a flat surface, wrong side up and work out the position of your rod pockets. From the finished length of the blind deduct 10 cm (4 in) plus the depth of your bottom border. Divide what is left by twice the number of rod pockets plus one. This will give you the distance (x) from the top of the bottom border to the first rod pocket.

6 Draw a line in pencil very lightly across the blind at this point. Measure up 5 cm (2 in) and draw another pencil line across. Measure up twice x from the last line and draw another two lines 5 cm (2 in) apart, and so on until you have drawn two lines for each rod pocket.

7 Fold the blind, right sides together, through the middle of the first pair of lines, press and machine stitch along the pencil lines, backstitching at either end, so that you form a 2.5 cm (1 in)-wide rod pocket. Repeat for all the other rod pockets. It is important that you do all this accurately so that your blind ends up the right length when all the pockets have been stitched, and that all the pockets are absolutely perpendicular to the sides of the blind so that it hangs straight when let down and pulls up evenly.

8 Fix the Velcro as described in step 5 on page 54. Then firmly sew on a brass ring onto either end of each rod pocket, just inside the border.

9 Cut the dowelling rods to the width of the blind less 3 cm (1¼ in), and insert one into each rod pocket. Stitch the ends of the rod pockets closed with removable tacking stitches.

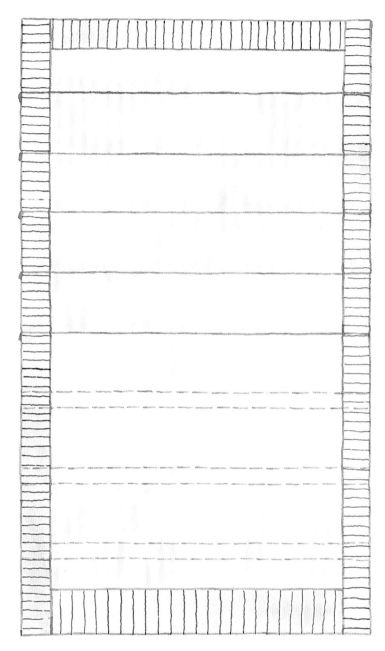

5, 6 & 7

10 Make a timber fixing as described in steps 7 and 8 on page 55, but do not insert a screw eye in the middle of it.

11 Finally, string up the blind as described in steps 9 and 10 on page 55.

techniques

STITCHES

SLIPSTITCH

Slipstitch is used for the hem of a curtain, or on two folded edges of fabric. Working from right to left, run your needle inside the folded edge for 1 cm (½ in) and then pick up a few threads of the face fabric so that the stitch is almost invisible. Where stitching together two folded edges, run the stitch inside the folded edge on one side for 1 cm (½ in), then cross over to the other folded edge and run it along inside for 1 cm (½ in). Although this stitch should be pulled through firmly, take care not to pull too hard or the fabric may pucker.

HERRINGBONE STITCH

This is a criss-cross stitch used to hold side hems on curtains and blinds and is worked from left to right. Secure the end of the thread, then take a tiny back stitch in the face fabric, catching only a couple of threads, before moving down and to the right to take a bigger back stitch through the folded fabric of the hem.

RUNNING STITCH TO ANCHOR ROD POCKETS TO FACE FABRIC

This is an elongated backstitch that runs directly beneath the rod pocket on the back of a Roman blind. Working from left to right, and using a double thread, anchor your thread securely at one side of the blind, just beneath the rod pocket. Take a tiny backstitch making sure that you catch the face fabric of the blind as well as the lining. Then move 7.5 to 10 cm (3 to 4 in) to the left before taking another backstitch.

BUTTONHOLE STITCH

This is used as a decorative stitch to bind the edge of a fabric and for handworked buttonholes. It is worked from right to left. Knot the thread and bring the needle out from the underneath, below the edge of the fabric to be worked. For each subsequent stitch insert the needle from the underside, looping the thread under the eye and the point of the needle. Pull the needle out of the fabric and away from you so that the knot that is formed sits on the edge of the fabric.

For buttonholes, the stitches are worked very close together and should be about 3 mm (⅛ in) deep. But for a decorative edge, they can be more spread out and enlarged (blanket stitch).

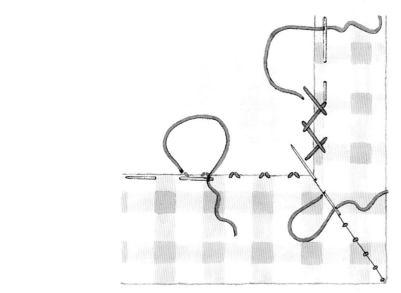

SLIPSTITCH AND HERRINGBONE STITCH

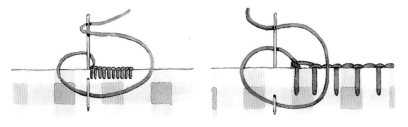

BUTTONHOLE STITCH

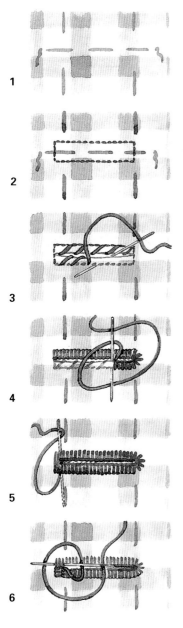

MAKING A BUTTONHOLE

BUTTONHOLES

1 Decide on the position and length of your buttonhole and mark it by tacking lines of running stitches down the centre and at either end.

2 With a very tiny stitch length, machine stitch a rectangle 6 mm (¼ in) wide by the length of the buttonhole opening plus 3 mm (⅛ in).

3 Cut along the buttonhole position line down the centre of the rectangle, from one end to the other, being very careful not to snip the machine stitches. Overcast the raw edges of the slit roughly to stop the fabric fraying while you work the buttonhole stitch.

4 Working from right to left along the edge of the slit that is nearest to you, work buttonhole stitches very close together (covering the machined rectangle which acts as a guide for stitch length) until that entire side is covered. When you reach the other end, fan about five to seven stitches around the end of the buttonhole, turning the work as you go and then proceed in the same way along the other side of the buttonhole.

5 When you have worked your way back to the beginning again, work a bar stitch by making several long stitches across both widths of buttonhole stitches.

6 For extra strength, you can work buttonhole stitches along each of the bar tacks, and fasten off your thread on the wrong side.

BIAS-CUT STRIP

Bias-cut strip is cut by taking the corner of a length of fabric and folding it over until the bottom edge of the fabric lies along the selvedge, making a diagonal

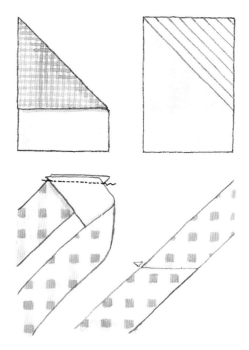

CUTTING AND JOINING BIAS-CUT STRIPS

fold across the fabric. Press along this fold and open it out to use the crease line as a guide and then mark parallel lines in chalk or pencil, spacing them the width of the strip you require (5 cm [2 in] wide for piping, wider for a bias cut border). Cut out enough strips so that, when they are joined, you have a continuous length long enough for the job in question.

To join bias-cut strips, with right sides facing, pin together two ends so that the strips are at right angles to each other. Stitch 6 mm (¼ in) in from the diagonal ends, along the straight grain and then press seams open.

PIPING

Piping cord can be bought in various sizes. Always buy it pre-shrunk. Cut enough bias-cut strips for your particular requirements and join them as shown above. Taking one end of the bias strip and one end of the cord, fold the fabric over the cord with wrong sides facing and

MAKING AND ATTACHING PIPING

aligning the raw edges of the fabric. Then, using a piping or zipper foot to the left of your needle, stitch close to the cord so that the cord is enclosed.

To apply piping to the edge of a cushion, for instance, the piping is applied in two stages. First it is stitched to the top piece of the cushion, and then the underpiece is stitched to both the piping and top piece (stitching through four layers of fabric). Each row of stitches is placed closer to the cord so that when finished, no stitching should be visible from the right side. To apply piping around a corner, clip into the piping seam allowance at the corner so that it opens out into a right angle. Stitch across the corners diagonally in order to blunt them.

Where two ends of piping meet, start by leaving a short length of piping free at the beginning of your run. When you get

back round to the beginning, cut the piping cord (but not the covering fabric) so that it butts up against the starting end of cord. Trim the fabric to 2.5 cm (1 in), fold under a neat hem and wrap it around the starting end so that the two ends of cord meet. Machine stitch across the join.

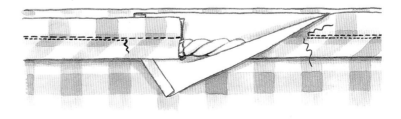

JOINING PIPING

DYEING TAPES

Tapes can easily be made from 2.5 cm (1 in) wide natural herringbone tape which can be bought in most haberdashers. However, sometimes it is necessary to dye them to match whatever you are making. For that particular project, the tapes were dyed to match the border by mixing three different dye colours and a bit of trial and error. Mix up small quantities of the dyes, keeping a note of the precise quantity of each colour, and immerse a short length of tape in the mixture for the required period. Then make sure your sample is completely dry before comparing colours (iron it dry between two thick layers of scrap fabric so you don't get dye on your iron or ironing board). If it isn't the right shade, try adding a bit more of the colour that you think is lacking. Try another piece of sample tape. Continue until you get as near to your border colour as you can.

You have to be systematic with this procedure so that you know which tape was dyed with which consistency of dye. When you have got it right, mix more dye with the same proportions of colours and dye all your tape.

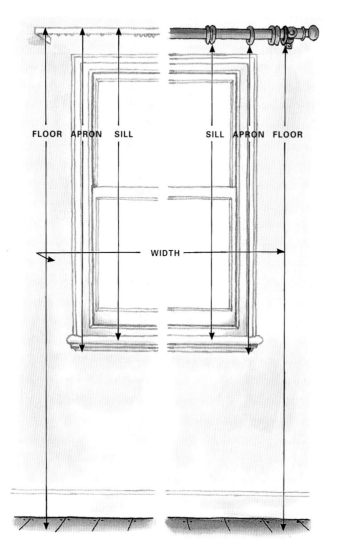

FLOOR APRON SILL   SILL APRON FLOOR

WIDTH

MEASURING UP FOR CURTAINS

MEASURING UP FOR CURTAINS AND BLINDS

Two measurements are needed to estimate the amount of fabric needed for curtains and blinds: the finished length and the finished width (see right). For the most accurate results, install your track or pole before you start making the curtains or blind. Then carefully measure using an extendable steel tape measure rather than a fabric measure.

FINISHED LENGTH

For curtains, measure from the top of your track, or the bottom of the wooden rings on a pole, to the required length – sill length, apron length or floor length. For floor length, if it is important that the curtains clear the floor subtract 1 cm (½ in) from your measurement. On the other hand, if you would like your curtains to break fashionably on the floor, add anything from 2.5 to 10 cm (1 to 4 in) to your measurement. Measure the length at several places across the width of the window to check for unevenness in the floor or window. If there is only a small difference, take an intermediate length; but if the discrepancy is large, you may have to make up the curtains, except for the hems, and hang them before pinning up the hems in situ.

For blinds, first decide on the position from where the blind will hang. For recessed windows, this is usually from the top of the recess (and the batten of the blind is screwed directly up into the recess). For flat windows, the batten is usually placed at the top of the architrave, or if there is a wide wooden frame, it can be set in lower down the frame, allowing some of the woodwork to be exposed. Once the position for the batten has been decided, the finished length is measured from the top of the batten to where the blind is to fall – usually sill length or just below.

FINISHED WIDTH

For curtains, measure the entire span of the track or pole. If the track projects out far from the wall, include the return (the distance it projects from the wall) at both ends in your finished measurement. Where possible, tracks and poles should extend at least 15 cm (6 in) on either side of the window to allow space for the curtains to hang when drawn back.

For blinds, measure the width of the area you wish the blind to cover: either the width of the recess, the width of the architrave, or narrower if you want some of the woodwork frame to show.

ESTIMATING FABRIC FOR CURTAINS AND BLINDS

FOR CURTAINS

Take the finished length measurement and add 20 cm (8 in) for the hem and 10 cm (4 in) for the heading.

If there is a pattern repeat in the fabric you have chosen, you will have to add an allowance for that. Divide your working length by the length of the pattern repeat. If the answer is a fraction, round it up to the next whole number and multiply that by the length of the pattern repeat. This will give you the full working drop.

To work out how many widths of fabric you will need in your curtains, multiply the finished width measurement by 1½ times, 2 times, 2½ times, or even 3 times, depending on your curtain heading, the weight of your chosen fabric and the amount of fullness you would like. Usually, allow 1½ times for very simple, narrow curtains; 2 to 2½ times for gathered, pencil pleated or pinch pleated headings; and 3 times for very fine muslin. Divide the resulting figure by the width of your chosen fabric (usually either 122 cm [48 in] or 137 cm [54 in]). Round that figure either up or down to the nearest whole number and that is the number of drops you will need.

For the total length of fabric required, multiply the full working drop by the number of drops.

FOR BLINDS

Take the finished length measurement, and add 5 cm (2 in) top and bottom for the hem and turning to work out the working length. Take the finished width measurement, and add 5 cm (2 in) either side for turnings to find the working width. Since the top of a blind is usually flat, to find out how many widths of fabric you will need, simply divide the working width by the width of your chosen fabric. If the resulting figure is less than 1, the total length of fabric required is the working length. If the result is more than 1, multiply the working length (if necessary, taking into account any pattern repeat – see left) by the number of widths to get the total length of fabric required. Alternatively, think about borders (see pages 66-9 for the study blind) or using a wider fabric.

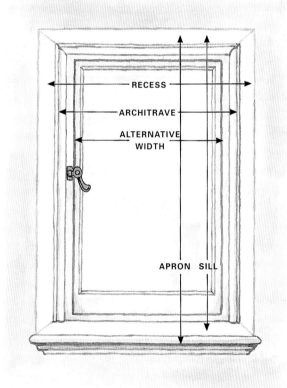

MEASURING UP FOR BLINDS

MITRING CORNERS

Mitred corners are used to make neat, flat corners without cutting away any fabric so that your hems can be let down at some later stage if necessary.

Press in the hem fold lines on both sides of your corner, and then open out the fabric so that it is flat again. Take the corner of the fabric and fold it in towards the centre until the diagonal fold line it forms crosses the point where the two pressed hem lines meet. Press the corner and then refold the hems so that a neat diagonal seam is formed. Slipstitch together the two folded edges.

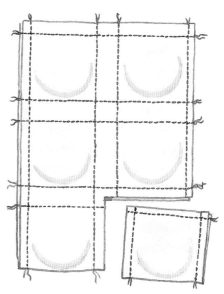

MAKING A LEAD WEIGHT COVER

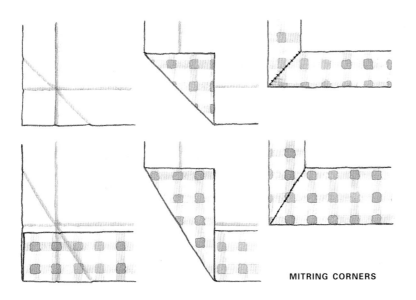

MITRING CORNERS

These instructions assume that the folded hems on either side of the corner are of equal depth. On the corner of a curtain hem, however, you may be trying to mitre a 10 cm (4 in) double hem to a 5 cm (2 in) single side hem. Press over the first 10 cm (4 in) hem of the double hem first and then proceed as above. To get the angle of the diagonal fold right, however, is a question of trial and error until the folded edges of the mitre meet in a neat seam.

LEAD PENNY WEIGHTS

Lead penny weights are available to buy in good soft furnishing departments. The easiest way to attach them is to make little pockets for them out of scrap lining fabric which can then be tacked to the curtain fabric inside the mitred corners and at the base of seams. The lining also prevents the weights from rubbing the face fabric.

To cover six weights, you will need a piece of scrap lining fabric measuring approximately 30 x 10 cm (12 x 4 in). Fold it in half, short end to short end, and machine a line of stitches about 5 mm (¼ in) in from each side so that you have a rough bag measuring about 15 x 10 cm (6 x 4 in). Now, machine two rows of stitching about 1cm (½ in) apart down the middle of the bag so that you make two channels into each of which you drop one weight. Machine two rows of stitching about 1cm (½ in) apart across the bag just above the weights. Drop in two more weights and continue as above until all the weights are enclosed. Cut off each pocket as you need them.

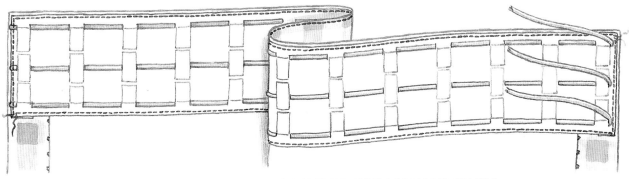

WIDE PENCIL PLEAT TAPE MAKES A STIFF AND REGULARLY PLEATED HEADING

CURTAIN HEADING TAPE

Curtain tape of different widths with pockets for curtain hooks and draw strings to gather up the curtains is bought by the metre (yard). There are several brands on the market, but experience shows that the more expensive brands are usually worth it because they form firmer and more neatly gathered headings. In the projects in this book we have only referred to two kinds of tape:

• 2.5 cm (1 in) gathering tape, which is usually set down 5 or 7.5 cm (2 or 3 in) from the top of the curtain to form an informal frill that will hide the hooks and curtain track from view. There is only one row of pockets for the hooks and two gathering cords.

• 7.5 cm (3 in) pencil pleat tape which makes a stiff and regularly pleated heading with three gathering cords and three rows of pockets for the hooks. This means that you can adjust the height of your curtain, depending on what mechanism you are hanging it from. The top row is for hooking to the rings of a curtain pole allowing the pole to be visible, and the middle or bottom rows are for hooking to a curtain track so that the track will be concealed.

To attach curtain tape to the top of your curtain, lay your curtain lining side up and position the tape close to the top edge (or to the marked line of your heading if it is to be set down from the top). The strings will eventually be pulled up on the outside edge of the curtain, so pull the strings out of the tape on the outside edge for 2.5 cm (1 in) and tuck under 1 cm (½ in) of tape and align to the outside edge of the curtain, leaving the strings free.

Machine along the top edge of the tape and when you get to the the leading edge, knot the strings off very firmly and tuck them under with the tape. Carry on machining around the end of the tape and backstitch when you reach the bottom. Return to the beginning, and machine down the other end, being careful not to catch any of the loose strings, and then machine around the corner and along the bottom edge of the tape, backstitching at either end.

Knot the loose strings together and then pull them up until the curtain heading measures the length of your pole or track, plus a little for ease (or you will find your curtains straining to meet in the centre when drawn). The most effortless way of pulling up very wide curtains evenly is to put the knotted end over a door handle and pull the curtain away from the door. Fasten the strings off with a slipknot (which will easily pull undone when required), wind the excess string into a neat skein and tuck it under the strings on the tape to keep out of view.

suppliers

All the fabrics used in the projects in this book can be bought from Ian Mankin's shops. He also supplies fabrics by mail order from the shop at Regents Park Road.

109 Regents Park Road
Primrose Hill
London NW1 8UR
Telephone: 0171 722 0997
Fax: 0171 722 2159

271 Wandsworth Bridge Road
London SW6 2TX
Telephone: 0171 371 8825

Ian Mankin's fabrics are also distributed by the following companies:

Europe
Compania de la India
Ortega Y Gasset 26
28006 Madrid
Spain
Telephone: 1 575 31 11

Chic & Bruk
Abbedikollen 28
0280 Oslo
Norway
Telephone: 22 733720

Chintz B
35 Rue de Rollebeek
1000 Bruxelles
Belgium
Telephone: 2 513 2269

Grupo 13
Ayala 54
28001 Madrid
Spain
Telephone: 1 435 1203

Holger Stewen
Hohe Bleichen 21
Hamburg 36
Germany 20354
Telephone: 40 35 16 09

Kompaniet
Blumenstrasse 23
80331 Munich
Germany
Telephone: 89 26 36 49

Mann & Rossi
Via 1
Ariosto 3
20145 Milan
Italy
Telephone: 2 48 01 18 10

Metre & Carre
2 Rue du 4 Septembre
30700 Uzes
France
Telephone: 4 66 22 45 12

Unicorn Diseno Interior
Carretera Palma Arte km 48
07500 Manacor
Baleares, Spain
Telephone: 71 55 56 62

Walles & Walles
Alstromergatan 20
11247 Stockholm
Sweden
Telephone: 8 650 1078

America
Agnes Bourne Inc
Two Henry Adams Street
Showroom 220
San Francisco CA 94103
USA
Telephone: 415 626 6883

Coconut Co
129/31 Greene Street
New York NY10012
USA
Telephone: 212 539 1940

Natural Textile Co Inc
4717 Piccadilly South
West Vancouver BC
V7W 1J8
Canada
Telephone: 604 925 6158

Far East
Larsens
14th Floor
Home Place Building
283/10 Sukhumvit 55
Klongton
Bangkok 10110
Thailand
Telephone: 2 712 7144

Decorative items

Aria
133 Upper Street
London N1
Telephone: 0171 226 1021
*(kitchenware, luggage and
other home items)*

Aria
259 Upper Street
London N1
Telephone: 0171 704 1999
*(bathroom items ranging
from wickerware to
toiletries – see photograph
on page 113)*

Bohemia
138 Regents Park Road
London NW1
Telephone: 0171 916 7690
*(furniture – see
photographs on pages 17
and 19)*

Christopher Farr
115 Regents Park Road
London NW1
Telephone: 0171 916 7690
*(rugs – see photograph on
page 17)*

Liberty
Regent Street
London W1
Telephone: 0171 734 1234
*(all items for the home –
see photographs on pages
35, 38-9 and 48-9)*

Meaker and Son
166 Wandsworth Bridge
Road
London SW6
Telephone: 0171 731 7416
*(furniture – see
photograph on page 77)*

George Pederson
152 Upper Street
London N1
Telephone: 0171 359 5655
*(see photographs on
pages 64 and 67)*

Peter Place at I and L
Brown Antiques
636 Kings Road
London SW6
Telephone: 0171 736 9945
*(wood and metal items –
see photograph on page 48)*

Summerhill and
Bishop
100 Portland Road
Notting Hill
London W11
Telephone: 0171 221 4566
*(kitchenware and items
for decorating kitchens –
see photograph on pages
38-9)*

Tidmarsh and Sons
Transenna Works
Laycock Street
London N1 1SW
Telephone: 0171 226 2261
*(custom-made fabric
blinds – see photograph
on page 95)*

David and Charles
Wainwright
22 Rosslyn Hill
Hampstead
London NW3
Telephone: 0171 431 5900
*(furniture and other
decorative items for the
home – see photographs
on pages 14-15 and 17)*

125

index

Page numbers in *italics* represent photographs
Entries in **bold** represent projects

Acknowledgments

The publisher thanks the following photographers and organizations for their kind permission to reproduce photographs in this book:

2 Clifford Studios; 5 Clifford Studios; 6 Robert Harding Picture Library / James Merrell / Homes & Gardens © IPC Magazines; 8 Clifford Studios; 10 Robert Harding Picture Library / Adam Woolfitt; 11 Robert Harding Picture Library / Jan Baldwin / Homes & Gardens © IPC Magazines; 17 Robert Harding Picture Library / James Merrell / Homes & Gardens © IPC Magazines; 28 Clifford Studios; 30 Robert Harding Picture Library / James Merrell / Options © IPC Magazines; 31 Elizabeth Whiting & Associates / Jean-Paul Bonhommet; 32-33 Elizabeth Whiting & Associates / Jean-Paul Bonhommet; 42 Clifford Studios; 44 Jacqui Hurst; 45 Clifford Studios; 56 Clifford Studios; 58 Marie Claire Maison / Marie Pierre Morel / Daniel Rozensztroch; 59 Robert Harding Picture Library / James Merrell / Homes & Gardens © IPC Magazines; 60-61 The Interior Archive / Fritz von der Schulenberg / Designer Mimmi O'Connell; 70 Clifford Studios; 72 Trip / M Feeney; 73 Robert Harding Picture Library / Geoffry Frosh / Country Homes & Interiors © IPC Magazines; 74-75 Robert Harding Picture Library / Chris Drake / Country Homes & Interiors © IPC Magazines; 92 Clifford Studios; 94 Agence Top / Martin Fraudreau; 96 Robert Harding Picture Library / Tom Leighton / Homes & Gardens © IPC Magazines; 104 Clifford Studios; 106 Jacqui Hurst; 107 National Magazine Company / SHE / Rosemary Weller; 109 Robert Harding Picture Library / Simon Brown / Country Homes & Interiors © IPC Magazines.

All other photographs © Nadia Mackenzie.

The publisher would also like to thank the following for supplying items for the photographs:
London Furniture Services, Windmill Works, Alma Road, Enfield, Middlesex EN3 7BE (Victorian campaign bed on page 47)
Henry Newbury & Co Ltd, 18 Newman Street, London W1P 4AB (soft furnishing trimmings on pages 98-9)
GJ Turners, Fitzroy House, Abbot Street, London E8 3DP (fringe on page 24-5)
Wild at Heart, Turquoise Island, Westbourne Grove, London W11 (flowers on pages 35 and 48-9)
Joshua Wiskey, telephone 0181 969 9093 (oil painting, page 62)